T0384057

Internalizing a Culture of Business Excellence

Perspectives from Quality Professionals

Internalizing a Culture of Business Excellence

Perspectives from Quality Professionals

By
Flevy Lasrado
Norhayati Zakaria

A PRODUCTIVITY PRESS BOOK

by Routledge/Productivity Press
52 Vanderbilt Ave. New York, NY 10017, USA
2 Park Square, Milton Park, Abingdon, Oxon OX14 4RN, UK

© 2019 by Taylor & Francis Group, LLC
Routledge/Productivity Press is an imprint of Taylor & Francis Group, an Informa business

No claim to original U.S. Government works

Printed on acid-free paper

International Standard Book Number-13: 978-0-8153-8117-4 (Hardback)

This book contains information obtained from authentic and highly regarded sources. Reasonable efforts have been made to publish reliable data and information, but the author and publisher cannot assume responsibility for the validity of all materials or the consequences of their use. The authors and publishers have attempted to trace the copyright holders of all material reproduced in this publication and apologize to copyright holders if permission to publish in this form has not been obtained. If any copyright material has not been acknowledged, please write and let us know so we may rectify in any future reprint.

Except as permitted under U.S. Copyright Law, no part of this book may be reprinted, reproduced, transmitted, or utilized in any form by any electronic, mechanical, or other means, now known or hereafter invented, including photocopying, microfilming, and recording, or in any information storage or retrieval system, without written permission from the publishers.

For permission to photocopy or use material electronically from this work, please access www.copyright.com (http://www.copyright.com/) or contact the Copyright Clearance Center, Inc. (CCC), 222 Rosewood Drive, Danvers, MA 01923, 978-750-8400. CCC is a not-for-profit organization that provides licenses and registration for a variety of users. For organizations that have been granted a photocopy license by the CCC, a separate system of payment has been arranged.

Trademark Notice: Product or corporate names may be trademarks or registered trademarks, and are used only for identification and explanation without intent to infringe.

Library of Congress Cataloging-in-Publication Data

Names: Lasrado, Flevy, author. | Norhayati Zakaria, 1969- author.
Title: Internalizing a culture of business excellence : perspectives from quality professionals / Flevy Lasrado and Norhayati Zakaria.
Description: 1 Edition. | New York : Taylor & Francis, [2019] | Includes bibliographical references and index.
Identifiers: LCCN 2018038425 (print) | LCCN 2018051468 (ebook) | ISBN 9781351210720 (e-Book) | ISBN 9780815381174 (hardback : alk. paper)
Subjects: LCSH: Total quality management. | Quality control. | Economic development. | Success in business.
Classification: LCC HD62.15 (ebook) | LCC HD62.15 .L377 2019 (print) | DDC 658.4/013--dc23
LC record available at https://lccn.loc.gov/2018038425

Visit the Taylor & Francis Web site at
http://www.taylorandfrancis.com

Contents

Foreword

Quality – one of the most overused words in organizations today. It has become fashionable for business leaders to say the word in passing every so often – it almost feels like without stating the word "quality" an organization's mission seems incomplete. As much as we like to throw the word around, do we as business leaders truly understand the meaning of quality? This contribution by Dr Lasrado and Dr Zakaria on *Internalizing a Culture of Business Excellence: Perspectives from Quality Professionals* gives business leaders and the broader community unique viewpoints on quality – from quality managers themselves! Dr Lasrado and Dr Zakaria give us an entirely different perspective for young professionals to think about as we begin to design the jobs of tomorrow – jobs that have not even been dreamt of yet. This book is essential in that it establishes the continued need to think of quality regardless of the transformations that are taking place around us.

We are fortunate that we now have such perspectives thanks to Dr Lasrado and Dr Zakaria's efforts. We must now continue to march on with the flag of quality and open up our boardrooms so that quality professionals occupy a seat at the table. Organizations that do this are the ones that will remain adaptable to the challenges that lie ahead.

The one thing we know for sure is that those challenges will be significant and will need us to adopt the lessons that are detailed in this book.

Navin Valrani
CEO
Education and Engineering Services
Oasis Investment Company (Al Shirawi Group)

Preface

In 25 years of excellence, the United Arab Emirates (UAE) has raised several quality professionals who are working to increase organizational competitiveness. Thankfully, we have a great trend and history to our excellence journey in the UAE. Rightly, as quality is evolving and we are embracing organizational excellence in the age of digital transformation, the role of quality experts is becoming increasingly important. It was, in fact, fascinating to see how our quality experts in the UAE are contributing to this mega-trend. Passion was the key element behind their profession; their journey gives interesting insights. The idea behind the collection was to spark a new debate on internalizing the quality. Are we ready for its internalization? Do we have a "culture" to support the internalization? True "quality" didn't remain as a luxury but rather a necessity; excellence is a way of life in the 21st century. The fundamental questions, therefore, will continue to raise how well prepared are we as quality professionals in the 21st century? How do we transform our organizations to sustain our competitiveness? Customer centricity and people focus are levers that are to be leveraged no matter what may come; finding a way to internalize them to our organizational culture is not only a challenge but also an opportunity to act upon.

Likewise, more important is to address the emerging question in the age of digital transformation for contemporary organizations: Why should an organization create a culture of quality? The answer is affirmative, with numerous reasons. One primary reason is to address the concerns of those organizations that aim to create sustainability by incorporating people, planet, and profit as the *three P*s bottom line. For example, societies will continue to seek and demand products and services that are quality-driven and align with their environmentally conscious minds and desires. As such, *Go Green* will be the key invocation among organizations to compete and rise above the mere profit motivation goals. Governments will be more alert and sensitive and thereby strike many more initiatives towards promoting awareness through campaigns. Introducing policies that establish stringent guidelines for organizations to comply and implement in their organizations will be the new reality. Additionally, suppliers will only collaborate with organizations that meet equitable "quality standards" and vice versa—organizations will only choose suppliers who are green-sensible, for example. Without a doubt, contemporary organizations who care about corporate social responsibility will frequently and continuously strive for business excellence.

Thus, how important is culture to an organization? In the context of organization, culture is the underpinning roots that result in shared values, attitudes, and beliefs that form the basis of the behavior of people. Culture also acts as the driver and influencer for any behaviors to take place. The next challenging question would thus be: How do organizations develop the culture of quality through the business practices of excellence? Wouldn't it be that if and when leaders strive for excellence, quality becomes the pillar for the formation of values and principles that consequently manifested in the people's behaviors? Thus, leaders have to make strategic decisions as to create a culture of inclusivity for all management levels to achieve quality and excellence. No exception for anyone in the organizations. All people must strive for quality. The meanings of quality must be equally shared, appreciated, and implemented. In essence, organizational culture is the engine of any organization. It allows people to understand the "way things are done," which creates the right and consistent values, perceptions, mental models, and attitudes of the people who belong to the same organization. In our book, we offer rich insights from quality professionals in the region who have demonstrated coherent values, appropriate skill sets, and superior competencies as well as best practices of how they have effectively performed, modeled out, and influenced their behaviors on to others that are aligned with the pillars of quality management. With this thought, it's a pleasure and honor to uncover emerging quality leaders in the region and to highlight their experience!

Dr. Flevy Lasrado and Dr. Norhayati Zakaria
Dubai, October, 2018

Acknowledgments

We would like to thank the Dubai Quality Award Office and all quality professionals for their time and effort in contributing to this first series of success stories. Each of our professionals have shared with us their unique experience, making this series a great collection for aspiring quality managers to learn from their counterparts. Indeed, it is often difficult to reach out to one and all, but the Dubai Quality Award office, Ms Shaikha Al Bishri, director of the Business Excellence Department, Dubai Economy and Ms Seema Sequeira, specialist of the Business Excellence Department, Dubai Economy rendered their timely help to identify these unique specialists. Our sincere gratitude and thanks to all.

Authors

Dr. Flevy Lasrado is a renowned academic and researcher at the University of Wollongong in Dubai (UOWD), where she oversees the Quality Management discipline. Dr. Lasrado has distinguished herself as an emerging author due to her strong, proven track record of making impactful contributions to both her academic and professional communities. To her credit, Dr. Lasrado has written five books published by renowned international publishers. Dr. Lasrado has received numerous awards and accolades. Her noteworthy success can be attributed to the fact that she has won several competitive research grants over the past few years, and her research has resulted in her achievement of the award of Research Excellence Award at UOWD. A passionate researcher, Dr. Lasrado has placed several global issues at the center of her research focus. In addition to her commendable research background, Dr. Lasrado volunteers in several community development projects and participates in assessment activities regarding excellence, innovation, and community welfare. Making her research accessible to both young minds and global business leaders, Lasrado has released impactful scientific articles that draw on her industry exposure to various projects and have also garnered competitive awards. At the 2014 World Quality Congress in Mumbai, Dr. Lasrado received a leadership award. Following this, an exceptional performance award and recognition for her partnerships at UOWD. In spite of her humble entrance into the realms of academia and research, today Dr. Lasrado stands out as a role model in academic excellence and accomplishment.

Dr. Norhayati Zakaria holds a PhD in Information Science and Technology and a MPhil of Information Transfer from Syracuse University, USA; an MS in Management from Rensselaer Polytechnic Institute, Troy, NY, USA; and a BBA in Human Resources Management from University Utara Malaysia. She is Associate Professor on the Faculty of Business and Management at the University of Wollongong in Dubai (UOWD), where she teaches courses in responsible leadership, intercultural applications for socially innovative business, and managerial concepts and skills. Her educational training bridges the interdisciplinary fields of cross-cultural management, international human resource management, international business, and computer-mediated communication technology. Her research program aims at exploring how and why cultural values shape people in terms of decision-making, negotiation, communication styles, leadership, and management practices. Her new research involves compiling cross-cultural tool kits for human resources training of global virtual teams. Her most recent book, *Culture Matters: Decision Making of Global Virtual Teams*, published by CRC Press, Taylor & Francis Group in 2017, marks her expertise in the integrated area of global human resources with technological savvy and cross-cultural competencies. She is currently engaged in another book project, *Culturally-Oriented Challenges for Self-Initiated Expatriates (SIEs) in Multinational Organizations*, which is expected to be published by Routledge in 2019. For over a decade, she has collaborated with global scholars from the United States, Japan, Malaysia, South Africa, and Canada. She has secured numerous international grants as Principal Investigator from the Asian Office of Aerospace Research Development as well as Co-Investigator from research grants such as the Japanese Society for the Promotion of Sciences, the Nippon Foundation, and the National Science Foundation. Some of her high-impact publications, indexed by ABDC, ISI, and Scopus, include: *International Journal of Management, Academy of Management and Learning Education, International Journal of Manpower, IT & People, The Database, Creativity and Innovation.*

Chapter 1

Internalizing Organizational Excellence: Why and How

The questions "What inspires people to delve into quality-related professions?" and "What do quality professionals think about?" are often on the minds of many people. A simple answer to these questions is that for these professionals, quality is the priority in everything they do. For them, quality begins within themselves as consumers, when they think to ask questions about any and all services and products. This mind-set is clearly a prerequisite for a quality professional.

Truly, quality has a great deal of scope; as Henry Ford put it, "Quality means doing it right when no one is looking." One implication of this is that quality has to be internalized at the personal level, and it has to be set within the DNA of ourselves and of the organization. So what is meant by the *internalization of quality*, and why is it important?

Introduction

Underlined by the importance of sustainable quality management practices to contemporary organizations, this edited
book compiles best-practice examples of quality professionals who have initiated and facilitated quality practices in
their organizations. The cases will highlight how these best
practices have manifested in their work cultures, values, and
beliefs. Not only do they address organizational efforts toward
the implementation of quality practices, but they also discuss
challenges leaders often face to instill a sense of quality practices across the hierarchical structures of their organizations.
Each chapter facilitates interesting and thought-provoking discussions in order to teach key quality concepts and to apply
relevant theoretical frameworks.

In today's business world, because transnational companies
face the dual challenges of managing global knowledge net-
works and multicultural project teams, as well as interacting
and collaborating across boundaries using global communication technologies, it is crucial to have quality management
programs in place that fit into these multicultural environments.
Although quality management may be viewed as both a cata-
lyst and driver for change, research has also clearly indicated
that national culture is highly resistant to change due to diverse
mind-sets, chaotic emotional challenges, and varying behavioral norms and patterns (Hofstede, 2001). In addition, although
quality practices can easily be changed, the fundamental values
that underlie those practices are very difficult to transform.
Such a phenomenon would suggest a strong need for global
firms to adapt their quality practices to the local national culture. As a consequence, the organizational cultures of globalized firms need to be aligned to the divergent values rooted
in the national cultures of the local leaders and workforces.
Accomplishing this cultural integration should not compromise the integrity of worldwide quality management policies;
rather, program development efforts should be geared toward

strategies that can be most effectively implemented in the local culture as well as the organizational culture. Thus, organizational leaders are increasingly in need of quality management approaches that will result in sustainable business practices.

Over the last few years, quality management and business excellence frameworks have been used extensively on the transnational scale to drive organizational performance. Indeed, managing quality is no longer a choice but a necessity to compete in highly globalized environments. The best practices of internalizing quality continue to evolve in this dynamic environment: organizations that continually adapt and learn from others thus manage to gain a competitive advantage. In the business world of today, with its diverse and multicultural workforce, it is important to learn from the best practices of companies in order to reap benefits in organizational performance, growth, and sustainability. This holds, in particular, for internalizing quality practices or organizational excellence.

Internalization: Why Is It Important?

Organizations have adopted several approaches to managing quality within their organization. Total quality management (TQM) is a well-known approach that many organizations use to monitor, control, and improve quality. Dozens of such programs have come into existence during TQM's evolution. Indeed, quality is still evolving, as there is no universal definition for managing quality. Various perspectives are therefore used to define quality that will guide its implementation. Because the quality is still evolving, one looming challenge for organizations today is to truly internalize these quality initiatives. Various internal and external pressures may bind an organization to adopting a management approach to quality, but to what extent this approach will truly help an organization to emerge as high performing truly depends on the internalization of the quality.

Simply put, internalization implies the adoption of the underlying practices of quality in their daily use by managers and employees alike (Link and Naveh, 2006; Darnall and Sides, 2008; Nair and Prajogo, 2009). Managers often find it challenging to create this mind-set, even after their organization has successfully obtained certification for attaining a level of quality recognition. Hence, the level of internalization in daily practice depends on the intensity of the internal and external motivations that the organization's managers and employees derive from such quality programs. Lasrado (2017), who studied the UAE context, listed several internal motivations and benefits that organizations generally perceive in a quality program. These include (1) the opportunity to benchmark, learn, share best practices, and improve processes; (2) the existence of a corporate image and market advantage; (3) the benefits experienced by others; (4) relations with communities and with the authorities; (5) customer pressure/demands; and (6) cost reductions.

While these factors help to reveal the benefits of adopting such programs, the encouragement for using these programs goes beyond simply recognizing the various factors in order to gain the crucial sustained performance of the organization. Through an empirical study of the various quality managers described in this book, several interesting insights are revealed about what drives their inspiration within the quality profession.

How Do We Internalize Organizational Excellence or Quality?

The next question that looms is how we internalize these practices. Studying this aspect of quality managers and leaders should help to present a number of strategies for internalizing a quality culture, including developing a passion for quality and internalizing quality at the personal level first. Lasrado

(2018) notes that a survey of quality managers meant to determine the extent to which employees use documentation in their daily routines observed that although it takes significant time to prepare the documentation, these routines are embedded within employees' daily work, and they motivate employees to become involved in quality initiatives. Organizations do often face difficulties in preparing the documentation, however, because of a lack of awareness about the standard itself, but involving employees in the process helps with this aspect in the long run. The organization-level documentation that is prepared as a result of quality initiatives is often utilized in the transformation of such initiatives into daily practices. Organizations mostly use these practices, which serve as a guide to quality culture. A number of factors can help in fostering the internalization of quality culture, including involving employees in the preparation of the documentation, providing adequate training in the usage of models, and integrating the requirements in the employees' daily routines.

Improving Internalization with AMO Theory

The ability, motivation, and opportunity (AMO) framework was assembled from a few basic concepts of psychology:

- Motivation: the impetus toward a behavior
- Ability: the skills and capabilities required for the performance of a behavior
- Opportunity: the contextual and situational constraints relevant to the performance of the behavior (Hughes, 2007)

The AMO framework was initially proposed by Bailey (1993), who suggested that ensuring employees' discretionary effort requires three components: employees must have the necessary skills and the appropriate motivation, and employers had to offer them the opportunity to participate (Appelbaum et al., 2000). Based on this model and drawing on the concept of high-performance work systems (HPWSs), the model was later developed by Appelbaum et al. (2000). According to the model, people perform well when they have the capability and adequate motivation, and when their work environment provides opportunities to participate (Boselie, 2010; Boxall and Purcell, 2007).

The ability dimension is usually further defined by knowledge, skills, and abilities (KSA) (Fu et al., 2013). Thus, ability-enhancing practices aim to improve those three components. Examples of these practices include employee recruitment techniques or formal training (Kroon et al., 2013). The motivation dimension has to do with an employee's desire to perform, which can be enhanced by extrinsic or intrinsic motivation. Examples of motivation-enhancing practices include incentives or career opportunities (Munteanu, 2014). Finally, the opportunity dimension considers not only individual characteristics but also the work environment, including practices such as quality circles or team-working exercises (Marin-Garcia and Tomas, 2016).

Taking all the this into account, as well as the importance of the AMO model and looking from various theoretical lenses of AMO theory, suggests that ability, motivation, and opportunity provide a basis for deep internalization. A question that should be asked related to the ability factor is, "What do employees experience being capable of?" Employees' experience can be elicited to enhance their ability to understand and master standards, which have to be deeply rooted within their work systems. Similarly, the second question that needs to be asked is: "What motivates employees, and which tasks specifically do they find meaning in?" Third, "Which opportunities do employees' experiences present?" Another question is, "What can managers do to improve ability, motivation, and opportunity to achieve internalization?"

Employees' abilities can be enhanced by developing their quality skills and experience in using standards. Employees' motivations to improve quality must be derived by directly involving them in the planning and implementing of quality initiatives; their roles or responsibilities should be embedded in the opportunities in order to improve their work systems. Managers should therefore focus on developing (1) ability-enhancing practices, such as building the awareness, training, and skills development of their employees in relation to quality standards, (2) motivation-enhancing practices, and (3) opportunity-enhancing practices in the form of employee involvement activities and the shaping of their job roles. Because organizational interests are best served by a system that attends to the employees' AMO factors, building these interventions should help to internalize the quality practice. Overall, AMO theory also suggests that three independent work system components shape employee characteristics and contribute to the success of the organization. Essentially, we utilize employees' abilities, desires, and opportunities to make a contribution to quality internalization.

The following chapters will explore specific quality and organizational excellence principles from the perspectives of several quality professionals.

References

Appelbaum, E., Bailey, T., Berg, P., and Kalleberg, A. L. (2000). *Manufacturing Advantage: Why High Performance Work Systems Pay Off.* London: ILR Press.

Bailey, T. (1993). *Discretionary Effort and the Organization of Work: Employee Participation and Work Reform since Hawthorne.* New York: Teachers College and Conservation of Human Resources, Columbia University.

Boselie, P. (2010). High performance work practices in the health care sector: A Dutch case study. *International Journal of Manpower, 31*(1), 42–58.

Boxall, P., Purcell, J., and Wright, P. (2007). Human resource management: scope, analysis, and significance. In *The Oxford Handbook of Human Resource Management* (p. 1). Oxford: Oxford University Press.

Fu, N., Flood, P. C., Bosak, J., Morris, T., and O'Regan, P. (2013). Exploring the performance effect of HPWS on professional service supply chain management. *Supply Chain Management: An International Journal*, *18*(3), 292–307. http://dx.doi.org/10.1108/SCM-04-2012-0118.

Hofstede, G. (2001). *Culture's Consequences: Comparing Values, Behaviors, Institutions and Organizations Across Nations*. Thousand Oaks, CA: Sage Publications.

Hughes, J. (2007). The ability–motivation–opportunity framework for behavior research in IS. In *40th Annual Hawaii International Conference on System Sciences, 2007* (*HICSS 2007*) (p. 250a). Washington, DC: IEEE.

Kroon, B., Van De Voorde, K., and Timmers, J. (2013). High performance work practices in small firms: A resource-poverty and strategic decision-making perspective. *Small Business Economics*, *41*(1), 71–91. http://dx.doi.org/10.1007/s11187-012-9425-0.

Lasrado, F. (2017). Perceived benefits of national quality awards: A study of UAE's award winning organizations. *Measuring Business Excellence*, *21*(1), 50–64.

Lasrado, F. (2018). *Achieving Organizational Excellence: A Quality Management Program for Culturally Diverse Organizations*. Cham, Switzerland: Springer.

Link, S. and Naveh, E. (2006). Standardization and discretion: Does the environmental standard ISO 14001 lead to performance benefits? *IEEE Transactions on Engineering Management*, *53*(4), 508–519.

Marin-Garcia, J. A., and Tomas, J. M. (2016). Deconstructing AMO framework: A systematic review. *Intangible Capital*, *12*(4), 1040–1087.

Munteanu, A. (2014). What means high performance work practices for human resources in an organization. *Annals of the University of Petrosani, Economics*, *14*(1), 243–250.

Chapter 2

Quality Culture at the Top: Insights from a Quality Leader

This chapter presents a profile of Mr. Sunil Thawani, a well-known figure in the field of Quality and Excellence in the United Arab Emirates. He will talk about his quality leadership journey. Thawani is known for developing leaders and for providing leadership to people, with a clear focus on results. Thawani is highly networked both locally and globally and is an engineer, MBA, and certified Six Sigma professional with over thirty-five years of leadership and management experience in marketing, sales, HR, operations, business transformation, customer engagement, continual improvement, performance management, developing and deploying strategy, and corporate governance, and he has worked in diverse industries such as manufacturing, oil and gas, logistics, services, government, consulting, banking, education, healthcare, real estate, and steel, among others. He is the recipient of the prestigious 2015 ASQ Lancaster Medal—the first recipient from the Middle East—for his dedication and outstanding contributions to the International Fraternity of Quality Professionals.

The American Society of Quality (ASQ) recognized Thawani as a Fellow in Quality and Excellence in 2009, which was a first from the Middle East and North Africa (MENA) nations. Thawani is the first Indian to have travelled around the world on motorcycle from 1984 to 1985 and has met Hon'ble Prime Ministers of India and the UAE and Ministers of the UAE, India, Slovenia, Ecuador, Lebanon, South Africa, etc. to help raise the Global Voice of Quality. He is currently serving as a Quality and Excellence Advisor to several organizations, including International Consultant for Quality And Excellence to the United Nations.

Profile: Sunil Thawani

For most people, job and joy are not one. For me, quality is one of my joys and passions. It excites me, it energizes me, it inspires me. It helps me make a positive difference in the lives of people, in the performance of organizations, and helps make this world a better place. Quality is a way of life for me. Until 1991, I had no idea about quality as a profession. One phone call changed the direction of my professional life. I was enjoying my work in marketing department of Bhilai Steel Plant, Steel Authority of India Limited (SAIL), in New Delhi, India. I was selected to appear for an interview for a position in the total quality management (TQM) Department, and, if selected, I would be sent to the USA for advanced training in TQM. Until that time, I had no idea what TQM was. In those days, there was no Google or Yahoo to search anything. Later on, I learnt that the TQM program was the brainchild of Dr. V. Krishnamurthy, then Chairman, SAIL. Dr. Krishnamurthy, truly a global visionary leader, was committed to creating a culture of Quality and Excellence in SAIL using TQM principles and philosophy. Those days in 1991, SAIL was an entity with about a quarter million employees, serving in about 60-plus Indian cities. As luck would have it, I got selected and went to visit

the excellent corporations and meet leaders of IBM, Corning
Glass, US Steel, Xerox Corporation, Boeing Corporation, etc.
Visits to these corporations and extensive training in TQM
principles, Malcolm Baldrige National Quality Award, process
management, reengineering, customer value management,
etc. was fascinating. Fast-forward 2–3 years, I got a break
and a wonderful opportunity to work with Mr. Janak Mehta,
Chairman TQM International Pvt. Ltd., New Delhi, India. In
the 1990s, Mr. Mehta set out with a missionary zeal to bring
TQM into the boardrooms of the Indian corporate world and
trigger Quality movement in Indian companies. Mr. Mehta is
a globally recognized Quality Leader and a great mentor. He
is my coach and I continue to learn and get inspired by him.
Fast forward to the UAE. I landed on the shores of Dubai in
the mid-1990s and since then have played an active part of
the UAE's Journey Towards Excellence in various roles such
as Team Leader and Sr. Assessor for the Dubai Quality Award
(DQA), Member of the Jury for the DQA and SKEA, Chairman,
Continual Improvement, Dubai Quality Group, Country
Counsellor for American Society for Quality, etc. Government
initiatives such as establishment of the Dubai Government
Excellence Program, Abu Dhabi Government Excellence
Program, Dubai Service Excellence Scheme, Sheikh Khalifa
Excellence Program, etc. brought Quality and Excellence to
the forefront of industry and caught the imagination of gov-
ernment and business leaders, Quality and other professionals.
All of this and much more provided me with a timely opportunity and helped me implement Quality and Excellence frameworks, models, quality strategies, and methodologies such
as the DQA Model (based on the European Foundation for
Quality Management [EFQM] model), MRM Business Model,
SERVQUAL, UAE 4th Generation Model, ISO standards (e.g.
9001, 10002, 14001, OHSAS 18001, etc.) in diverse industries,
solve complex business problems and develop sustainable
solutions. I enjoyed shaping, transforming, and building organizations to be become highly customer focused, continually

improving, and differentiated in the marketplace for delivering excellence.

With the UAE's growing and diversifying economy and high competition, I started to apply quality tools and techniques such as reengineering, benchmarking, service excellence, service standards, mapping customer journeys, enhancing customers' experiences, etc. in different industries. Though each industry is unique and has its own characteristics, they also experience a similar set of problems of process management, customer focus, agility, people engagement, culture of quality, continual improvement, etc. It was a great learning experience for me.

Some of the highlights of my work are that I (1) created a culture of cost consciousness, excellence, improvement, performance management, and customer focus; (2) led the development of policies and a process management framework to execute strategies; (3) developed and implemented a five-year road map to excellence; (4) provided leadership to a team for implementing an excellence framework (the EFQM model) and the SERVQUAL model, both of which yielded exceptional results; (5) attained certifications for international standards such as ISO 9001, 14001, 18001, and 10002; (6) won prestigious awards like UN Public Service Award (the first ever for an Abu Dhabi government entity), SKEA Gold (with the highest score to that date), DQA, MRM, UAE 4th Generation; and (7) launched continual improvement programs at the organization-wide level using Lean, reengineering, and kaizen techniques, which led to significant improvements in quality, cost, time, deliveries, and customer satisfaction.

Other core areas of my expertise include corporate governance. I have established board-level committees (nominations, audit, remunerations, etc.), adopting the International Finance Corporation (IFC) framework for corporate governance in family-owned businesses. I have also planned, assessed, and improved organizational structures, policies, processes, and authority levels to conform to international best-practice governance models such as the OECD prin-ciples of governance. I have used assessment reports to drive improvements—for example, by strengthening controls and minimizing risks—and I have established management and measurement systems that have led to enhanced transparency, accountability, and performance.

As demand for quality professionals grew, universities, colleges, etc. started offering TQM and Excellence related courses and degrees. Moreover, many young people, includ-ing Emiratis, have now made quality their profession. With this, I started visiting universities on regular basis to share my experience, e.g., in University of Wollongong in Dubai, Bhilai Mahila College, India, American University of Beirut, Lebanon, Shoolini University, India, etc.

I love to coach, mentor, and train people. I share my knowledge freely and help people succeed. Over the last 25-plus years, I have trained hundreds of professionals in many parts of the world—India, the UAE, Oman, Bahrain, Mauritius, Nigeria, etc.—covering wide spectrum of qual-ity models, strategies, and tools, such as ISO standards, the EFQM model, benchmarking, service excellence, Lean, kai-zen, process management, reengineering, etc. In addition to the aforementioned, I also love to write. Over the years, I have published more than 50 papers, articles, and case stud-ies in many journals, publications, and newspapers, including authoring a book, in the year 2009, titled *Business Excellence Awards: Strategies for Winning*, which was released by H.E. Sheikha Lubna bint Khalid bin Sultan Al Qasimi, then Hon'ble Minister of Planning and Economy, UAE.

I have also travelled around the world, sharing experiences in conferences, universities, professional associations, semi-nars, World Quality Day, in countries like Hong Kong, Saudi Arabia, Bahrain, Mauritius, Canada, India, Oman, Slovenia, Nigeria, Iran, Sweden, the UAE, etc.

In 2005–2006, I visualized that soon the UAE would move towards a knowledge-based economy. It was time to bring in global best practices and resources to the UAE. The ASQ was best positioned to provide such resources for the UAE and beyond. As ASQ Country Counsellor in the UAE, I invited the leadership of the ASQ to the UAE in 2009–2010. ASQ is an about 70-year-old organization with 70,000-plus members in 135-plus countries. ASQ Leaders such as Mr. Robert Chalker, then ASQ Global Managing Director, Mr. Stephen Hacker, Chairman, ASQ, etc. visited the UAE and realized the huge potential for Quality and Excellence in the region. As Member of ASQ Global Advisory Committee and Member, ASQ Strategy Planning Group, I played an important role in bringing ASQ's global vision to reality by starting the ASQ MEA office in Dubai, the UAE.

To enhance the competencies and skills of quality professionals in the UAE, in 2002–2003 I started proctoring and organizing ASQ certification exams in the UAE. This has helped hundreds of professionals in the UAE and neighboring nations to be certified in many of the 20-plus quality-related certification programs offered by ASQ.

As the rate of improvement decides the winner in market place, it was very important to establish, help, and inspire people and organizations to embark on a journey of continual improvement. In 2007–2008, as Chairman, Continual Improvement Group (CIG) of DQG, I, along with Mr. Prashant Nasery (Secy. CIG) and team, established a Continual Improvement and Innovation conference wherein organizations presented their case studies on improvement and innovation. Best practices with people were recognized. Currently, the conference is in its 10th/11th year and is one of the most successful and sustainable initiative of DQG in the UAE.

Since the dawn of century, human life has been dependent on quality. Quality has helped make products and services safer, more reliable, affordable, comfortable, enjoyable, etc. Therefore, it is very important to recognize "hidden" soldiers such as quality technicians, quality auditors, Lean Six Sigma experts, professors, managers, directors, and leaders, etc.

who work tirelessly to lead and implement quality. Towards this end, in 2015, I, along with Ms. Nancy Nouaimeh (current Chair, LMC, ASQ), developed the first ever ASQ UAE Quality Professionals Award and in the year 2016 developed and launched the first ever ASQ UAE Team Innovation Award. As member of the Award Jury, I am pleased to see real heroes being appreciated and recognized in the community.

ASQ develops Member Leaders. I am fortunate to be one of them. ASQ has always strongly supported me in my development, helped me perform my role in an effective manner, and also enhanced my role from national to global level. From 2016 to 2017, I have been fortunate to be selected to serve as Member, ASQ Board of Directors, the first ever person from Middle East and Africa to serve on the ASQ Board. This provided me with the unique and great opportunity to learn the Global State of Quality, strategize ASQ's global expansion through the World Partner Program, and shape the future of our ASQ society.

Learning is an ongoing process. I am a lifelong student of teachings of Dr. W. Edwards Deming, Dr. Jospeh Juran, and Prof. K. Ishikawa, etc. I have had opportunity to listen, learn, meet, and interact with some of the world's leading authorities on Quality and Excellence such as Mr. Phil Crosby, Dr. James Harrington, Dr. Hitoshi Kume, Dr. Noriaki Kano, and Dr. Yoshio Kondo, among others.

Since government provides and regulates services for millions of people and I have worked in the government for a long time, I realized the importance of service quality in the design and delivery of services and operational excellence. To improve services, transparency, governance, accountability, etc., the United Nations have established the UN Public Services Award, and 23rd of June is dedicated as Public Service Day. I had the opportunity to participate in UN Public Service conferences in South Korea, Holland, Bahrain, and Oman, etc. This made me learn more about service quality issues experienced by people, governments, and nations around the world. I became more aware about United Nations Sustainable Development Goals 2030 framework (UNSDGs). This humbling and inspiring experience made me commit to get actively involved in UNSDGs and make them famous. I see a huge opportunity for quality professionals to get involved in and make a positive difference.

Conclusion

Having a passion for quality is the key to success. Quality is all about people and their passions. The late Dr. Joseph Juran (1904–2008), Quality Guru, rightly said, *"Quality professionals thank your lucky stars as your field will only grow."* He was right. With the United Nations Sustainable Development Goals 2030 framework, we the quality professionals have a unique, global, and wonderful opportunity to give our Gift of Quality to UNSDGs.

We can get involved with UNSDGs in many ways. (1) Become a Goalkeeper (choose a UNSDG of our choice); (2) commit our time; (3) share our skills and knowledge with governments, partners, and other stakeholders; (4) make Goals more famous; (5) help build competencies in quality tools in community; (6) help raise financial resources; (7) influence government policies and programs; (8) mobilize corporations to get involved in SDGs; (9) collaborate on an ongoing project, etc. We all can make this world more sustainable with No One Left Behind.

Reflecting back, I never planned my life's quality leadership journey. It is a result of opportunities, passion, learnings, dedication, and the help and blessings of my dear family, friends, colleagues, peers, and students. I feel blessed.

Thank you for the opportunity.

Chapter 3

New CRM Acronym – "Customer Really Matters"

This chapter presents a profile of Satish Kaul, a quality expert based in the UAE. Satish voices his passion for quality and emphasis on customer centricity. Satish made significant improvements in his workplace—in particular, making the customer really matter in customer relationship management (CRM). He briefly details several quality initiatives and methodologies in his excellence drive with specific guidance on merging quality professionals.

Introduction

Backed by thirty years of experience in the areas of manufacturing and service quality, I was inspired to be a quality management leader for several reasons.

A quality and business excellence initiative not only energizes the organization and its leaders but also involves them in monitoring and reviewing the progress to chase the goals relentlessly once decisions are taken. Quality management emphasizes the core aspects of the creation of strategies, systems, and procedures as well as people development, communication, and knowledge sharing, among other things.

Companies over the years have adopted a host of excellence models and approaches to improving the quality and efficiency of their output, such as business process reengineering, Lean Six Sigma, total quality management, and business process management, among others. These proven methodologies provide a valuable framework with which to assess organizational performance on a wide range of key business indicators pertaining to factors such as customers, products, services, and operational and financial processes.

Quality management initiatives have encouraged me to interact better with my peers and perform my tasks more efficiently as a professional. Besides equipping employees with the necessary resources and giving them the freedom to strive for excellence, quality management initiatives have helped me to ascertain stakeholders' needs, coach employees, measure and reward good performance, and recognize contributions. Being proactive, fostering open and honest communication, and developing trust among teammates have been the added advantages of following the initiatives.

Quality management emphasizes three main pillars for the continued success of any organization: the voice of the customer, the voice of the people, and the voice of the process. How does one unravel and tap the value from each of these pillars?

Quality is a journey with no finishing line. In the domain of quality, there are no overnight results; a quality professional has to be determined and forbearing. Over the years, quality has taught me to be patient, be what I am, know my subject well, be analytical and straightforward, and follow the principles. Quality is a tough route, and I have learned over the years that with the appropriate subject knowledge, a positive attitude, and a good combination of hard and soft skills, people can accomplish quality initiatives in their respective careers.

Quality proficiencies include experience with quality management systems such as ISO 9001, ISO 14001, OHSAS 18001, ISO 10002, ISO 22301, and so on; business excellence models; awards such as the European Foundation for Quality Management (EFQM) Excellence Award, the Dubai Quality Award, and the Sheikh Khalifa Excellence Award; the seven quality control tools; and Six Sigma.

Process reengineering and quality proficiencies also include expertise in competency evaluation and developmental planning, sustainability reporting, customer satisfaction/mystery shopping surveys, and total product management.

The Focus: Customer Centricity

Coming back to the subject of pillars, the first and foremost area of quality is customer centricity, which implies putting customers at the center of the enterprise and aligning strategies and actions for a strong relationship to be nurtured over a period of time. Doing repeat business with the organization underscores customer centricity as much as the key elements of understanding customer value proposition, defining service intent, and deploying the required initiatives and products and services to the customers.

Customer centricity assumes the highest significance in today's highly competitive business environment. One needs to manage the expectations of different stakeholders, the most demanding of whom is the customer.

As a professional, I feel business leaders should focus on bringing customer centricity from the periphery of an enterprise to the core in order to achieve the organization's vision and mission. Business leaders should walk the talk, lead by example, have the right people in the right positions, and empower and support their employees to realize the organization's goals. Almost all companies have similar products, but it is service and quality that differentiates the good from the bad. Leaders/CEOs should ensure that customers are given exceptional service consistently, to prevent them from drifting toward competitors.

My exclusive experience, as illustrated below, highlights the customer centricity approach applied in one of my organizations. The entire customer focus approach is described in Customer Really Matters and the five key questions around it.

Five Key Questions

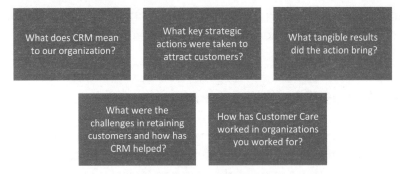

What Does CRM Mean to the Organization?

Let us begin the answer to this question with a famous quote by Mahatma Gandhi:

> A customer is the most important visitor on our premises. He is not dependent on us. We are dependent on him. He is not an interruption in our work. He is the purpose of it. He is not an outsider in our business. He is part of it. We are not doing him a favour by serving him. He is doing us a favour by giving us an opportunity to do so.

With this backdrop and inspiring thoughts, for us, Customer Really Matters (CRM) is a key business strategy that will determine the success of the organization. Customer Really Matters signifies ascertaining, meeting, and exceeding customer requirements at every phase of his/her life cycle with the organization. These phases are broadly categorized into five distinct stages: reach, acquisition, conversion, retention, and loyalty/advocacy. A proper and efficient management of expectations throughout the various stages of the customer life cycle results in an increased customer lifetime value (CLV). CLV is the total value or net profit generated by a customer for an organization across the entire customer lifecycle. A long and enduring relationship with the customer not only results in a higher CLV but also yields customer advocacy—that is, the customer acting as an ambassador for the organization, thereby supporting and referring the company's products and services to others.

Customer Really Matters is about companies not just spending a fortune upgrading their systems but also equipping and empowering their people to pay attention to customer needs during the presale, sale, and after-sale stages. Happy customers are the vital ingredient of any successful business, which again underscores Customer Really Matters. Customer Really Matters helps to improve customer satisfaction and loyalty, as the customer receives services that are in line with their expectations.

Strategic Actions: How to Attract Customers

According to global research, the cost of transforming an active customer into a loyal customer is lowest when the customer's requirements are consistently met and exceeded. This is essential as the cost of acquiring a new customer is approximately five times more than that of retaining an existing customer.

Some of the key strategic actions implemented over the years to retain and attract new customers are as follows:

■ Implementation of a CRM software tool: The aim is to reach out effectively to current and potential customers through focused/informed products and services. This means not only adopting technology but also taking a 360-degree view of the customer and outlining a strategy to reach out to customers in a uniform manner.

■ Introduction of alternate delivery channels: These include online banking, mobile banking, digital wallets, and ATM banking, thereby increasing customer convenience and the speed of service.

■ Provision of a wide range of products and services: This allows customers to choose a product/service from a basket of offerings that match their needs.

■ Launching product bundling: A strategy that offers creative bundling solutions—for example, free suffix accounts to the main account, an automatic line of credit with mortgage finance, and credit cards with a host of benefits.

■ Preapproved products: Issuing preapproval letters for credit cards, lines of credit, or mortgages for customers who have a good credit history and a positive spending trend with the bank.

■ Referral programs: Both staff and customers are encouraged to refer a friend/relative/colleague and earn reward points. Frontline staff who interact with the majority of bank clientele are oriented on both cross-selling and up-selling techniques and also looking for opportunities for customer referrals.

■ Personalized services for high net worth and private banking clients: Dedicated relationship managers focus on finding the best solutions to fit complete financial scenarios.

■ Superior customer service: In the pursuit of excellence, special courses have been designed for customer-facing staff, who are regularly trained on the intricacies and nuances of excellent customer service. Key facets include dedication to customer satisfaction, providing an immediate response, no buck-passing, going the extra mile to serve the customer, timely delivery, keeping promises, and the error-free delivery of services.

■ Reconnecting with dormant customers: Reconnecting with dormant customers with reliability and resilience will make them more receptive to reactivating their relationship with the bank, as they are familiar with the products, services, and practices. By overcoming their concerns and demonstrating a sense of trust and respect, this will lead to growth in revenues and customers becoming loyal advocates.

Strategic Actions: The Tangible Results

Some of the prominent results achieved due to the strategic actions taken to attract customers are as follows:

■ With a CRM tool in place, a proper history of the customers' profiles and offers made, and discussions with customers recorded and made available to all stakeholders, there was an explicit alignment in the delivery of services, products, and solutions to customers serviced by different staff at various touch points (branch, call center, etc.).
■ Focused cross-selling and up-selling efforts were made by the service staff by making appropriate offers to the customers through their preferred channel of interaction.
■ Through CRM-intelligent sales, marketing strategies were able to be formulated since the organization had a better understanding of which customers to target along with suitable solutions/offerings.
■ Substantial cost savings were achieved as customized solutions/offerings addressing customers' specific needs were developed and provided through the right channels.
■ Improvements were observed in staff productivity due to the accessibility of information, better accuracy, and the reduction of rework.
■ Increases in customer satisfaction and customer loyalty scores were observed due to the provision of a wide

range of products and services, the availability of alternate delivery channels, and smarter and faster uses of technology (e.g., mobile applications).

■ Growth in service quality scores were observed due to the regular training of frontline staff on superior customer service, cross-selling, and other soft skills.

■ More efficient customer profiling was achieved, including demographic, geographic, and psychographic characteristics, and customer buying patterns, purchase histories, and creditworthiness. This also improved the availability of easier and superior MIS reports on sales productivity, product profitability, customer profitability, and so on.

Challenges in Retaining Customers: The Role of CRM

The biggest challenge faced by the banking/financial industry in retaining customers is managing changing customer expectations. In the current era of rapid technological development, customers expect simple, fast, and user-friendly experiences from financial institutions, similar to the expectations they have when interacting with technology giants such as Apple and Amazon.

Another challenge for the banks/financial institutions is increasing competition. Now that the brick-and-mortar type of banking has been replaced to a greater extent with online and other delivery channels, the banks' target customers and competitive markets are no longer defined by geography but predominantly by banking regulations, the use of advanced technology, and advertising budgets.

The third challenge is developing innovative products and ways to serve the customer better. Financial institutions are investing heavily in product innovation related to digital channels. Similarly, information technology spending across banks is exploding.

With the introduction of CRM tools, the following benefits will help the business succeed:

■ Provision of a comprehensive analysis of marketing, sales, and services support for the easy integration of processes and the better alignment of staff in having common goals across the organization.
■ Better availability of robust data on the effectiveness of various communication channels/advertisements launched to retain/attract customers.
■ Help in the generation of extra revenues due to increased cross-sales.

CRM provides the key components required for an effective cross-selling program, as follows:

■ Technology component: A comprehensive database and analytical tools that allow deep understanding of each customer.
■ Process and incentive components: An enterprise-wide cross-sell system with incentives that drive user confidence and behavior.
■ Training and workflow components: Trained representatives delivering the right message at the right time to customers.
■ Knowledge management components: A feedback loop that builds on the knowledge gained to produce more effective contacts in the future.

Importance of Customer Care Management

Over the years at the organizations where I have worked, the voices of customers and ascertaining customer needs have assumed significant importance and played dominant roles in strategic and tactical business-making decisions.

The current banking industry is in the middle of a multi-wave trend encompassing digitization to optimize products and services, big data analysis to target more customers, and the offering and leveraging of technology and innovation to be more customer-centric.

An effective and successful customer care management program is a holistic framework that focuses on listening and acting on customer feedback throughout the customer lifecycle—that is, during the presale, sale, and after-sale stages. Great organizations always value customer feedback/complaints, as they provide an opportunity to analyze and improve products and processes and also enhance customer relationships. Moreover, complaints provide valuable data for analysis and improvement; they are not for fault finding.

During my tenure with various organizations, the customer feedback management process has been repeatedly augmented from the customer perspective by following and embedding international best practices, so as to ensure effective and faster resolutions to customer feedback. Some of the good practices and initiatives undertaken over the years to make customer care programs robust are as follows:

- Customer feedback management is essential to the organization's strategic plan and should be included in the objectives of senior management and other relevant stakeholders.
- Having a well-defined customer care policy, which is made available to all stakeholders and uploaded to the company's website, thereby demonstrates organizational commitment to customer care.
- Providing multiple channels to customers to register their feedback encourages them to provide feedback directly to the organization in cases of dissatisfaction rather than sharing their experience with others.
- The use of an automation system for recording feedback lowers the risk of not recording customer feedback and

helps to improve the trend of compliance to customer feedback resolution times.

■ Clear and concise communication is important so that the clients are kept informed during the entire life cycle of feedback management.

■ Regular reviews are conducted on customer complaints processes, trends, and major causes. Corresponding action plans are undertaken during management review meetings and shared with senior management.

■ Staff competence is enhanced through training in complaint processing, automation systems, products and services, and soft skills such as how to handle irate customers and how to manage stress.

■ Service recovery is utilized to win back complaining customers. Staff at various levels are empowered to resolve complaints/feedback at the first point of contact, and this leads to increased customer satisfaction scores.

■ Compliance with internationally recognized management systems such as ISO 9001 (quality management systems) and ISO 10002 (complaints handling) are foundational for assuring high customer satisfaction, delivering best-quality support services, and making continuous improvements.

Personal Career Anecdotes

Keeping Up with Quality

This story may sound funny, but it is my real life experience. While working for a multinational company as a regional technical and quality manager (RTQM), I was looking after the quality and technical aspects of a few beverage manufacturing plants in India. I used to report to the regional vice president (RVP), under whom the regional finance manager, regional HR manager, regional supply chain manager, and a few others also used to work. I remember it was the month of April in India and the hot summer was knocking at the door. In my capacity as RTQM, I had a meeting with my supervising RVP on the dwindling quality scores of some of the beverage manufacturing plants. I had gone prepared with all the relevant information and action plans. I expected my boss to lend me an ear so that we could work toward the improvement of product quality. I had high expectations, but all my hopes were dashed when my boss brushed away my concerns, including the action plan, saying, "Mr. Koul, Please don't disturb my sales strategy for another three months."

At the time, I did not realize what he meant, but after reflecting on the statement, I gathered he was only keen on increasing his sales figures, selling products by any means. Over the next three months, from April to June, when the temperature hovered at a scorching 45 degrees Celsius or above, he dumped the products into the market regardless of their low quality. After May, as the sales pressure subdued owing to relatively cool weather, he took note of the low product quality, called for a meeting, and suggested the hiring of an external consultant to identify the reasons for the low-quality scores. I was very perturbed by his decision and raised my voice against it.

After my initial meeting with him in April, I had kept the corporate quality head and other important stakeholders including my RVP informed about the low-quality scores and proposed an action plan to enhance them. I had done my homework. When I mentioned my communication with the corporate quality head and other important stakeholders to the RVP, he was taken aback, as he had not paid proper heed to this action plan earlier. He called a meeting of all the relevant plant and quality managers and instructed them to follow the proposed improvement action plan in letter and spirit. This ultimately resulted in saving considerable amounts of money for the organization and led to the empowerment of plant executives to oversee the implementation of strategies and the improved results thereof.

Building and Maintaining Quality

My latest contribution to the quality and excellence success stories can be attributed to the efforts that I have made in my organization over the past few years. The credit for my achievements rests solely on my organization's CEO. His vision of excellence, his conviction for quality, and the "can do" attitude that he has ingrained among his staff have been the driving force behind my contributions.

I was instrumental in bringing about a paradigm shift in the banking sector in the UAE by having a buy-in from my management to move from regulation- and compliance-driven processes to stewardship processes and voluntary protection practices, especially in the domains of quality and business excellence. This resulted in the implementation of an integrated management system (IMS) comprising three standards at my organization: ISO 9001 (quality management systems), ISO 14001 (environmental management systems), and OHSAS 18001 (occupational health and safety management systems).

In 2011, these initiatives led the bank to earn the distinction of being the first commercial bank in the world to be certified for an IMS covering three standards. Since then, there has been no looking back. The other divisions in the bank were motivated and adopted the changes too, giving birth to a new organizational culture. As a result of these changes, the bank acquired certifications for ISO 27001 (information security), ISO 20000 (IT service management), ISO 26000 (social responsibility), ISO 10002 (complaints management), and recently, ISO 22301 (business continuity).

The spirit of continual improvement led to the migration of the best practices of IMS implementation across other subsidiaries of the bank in the UAE and overseas. I played a pivotal role in infusing a culture of excellence across the bank by incorporating the best practices and the initiatives derived from participation in various business excellence awards. Our organization is the only bank in the UAE to receive the SKEA Diamond Award twice, the DQA Gold Award once, and the MRM Business Excellence Award three times.

Further, in its quest to be a socially responsible organization, the bank initiated sustainability reporting from 2011 and has been publishing its sustainability key performance indicators (KPIs) every year. The bank's sustainability report published in 2015 followed the G4 guidelines of the Global Reporting Initiative (GRI). Additionally, the bank was awarded the CSR Label from the Dubai Chamber in 2015 and 2016.

Over the years, my organization has built a reputation as a secure bank with prudent policies and strong financial performance on a consistent basis. From a stand-alone bank at the turn of the century, it has grown into a group entity within the UAE and spread across the region.

Following best practices, our management in Egypt was keen to implement the IMS comprising ISO 9001, ISO 14001, and OHSAS 18001. I visited the Egypt operations in February 2015 and made a presentation to senior management on the advantages of the IMS framework, the rollout process, and the resource requirements, among other things, with the aim of having their buy-in. I followed up with a series of awareness sessions with the departmental heads and the core IMS implementation team. Simultaneously, I introduced the concept of roadshows for other relevant stakeholders such as the staff of Quality Management Services, Health and Safety, and Facility Management Services, among others. These steps eventually kick-started the IMS implementation processes in the Egypt operations.

I held the Egypt teams' hands and guided them through the certification process. The Egypt operation was certified to the IMS by LRQA in September 2015, becoming the second commercial bank in the world to do so.

Successful Methodologies

There are many useful quality models that can be applied to evaluate and improve the components of a particular system. To single out one quality model may be a tedious process and probably is not the right approach. I found the following models more appropriate and superior in the domains of service quality and business process improvement (Figure 3.1).

SERVQUAL

SERVQUAL, also referred to as the service quality gap model, is used by many industries across the globe to ascertain gaps in service quality. This model helps the organization to identify gaps between customer expectations and actual services

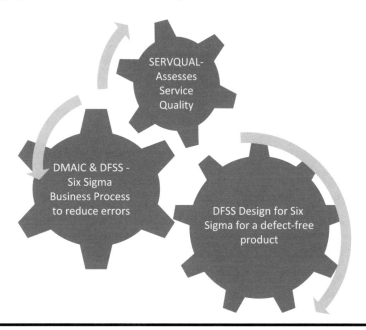

Figure 3.1 Models for service quality and business processes. (From A Parsu Parasuraman, Valarie A. Zeithaml, and Leonard L Berry. 1985. A Conceptual Model of Service Quality and its Implication for Future Research. With permission.)

provided at the different stages of service delivery. This is done by ascertaining the perceptions of a service along the five dimensions that represent service quality: reliability, assurance, tangibles, empathy, and responsiveness. This model enables the assessment of service quality from the customer's perspective.

DMAIC and DFSS for Business Process Improvement

Data-driven DMAIC (Define, Measure, Analyze, Improve, and Control) is an integral part of the Six Sigma business process improvement methodology. DMAIC focuses on bringing about improvements to the existing products and services of an organization by reducing the number of defects and errors. DMAIC is based more on manufacturing or transactional processes.

Design for Six Sigma (DFSS)

Aims at designing new defect-free products or services to meet critical-to-quality factors for customer satisfaction. DFSS includes aspects such as marketing, research, and design. The benefits and savings of DMAIC are quickly quantifiable, while those of DFSS are visible only in the long term.

Shaping the Future for Quality Professionals and Leaders

Quality professionals should not run with the hare and hunt with the hounds—that is, support both competing sides in a dispute and try to appease each side. Quality professionals need to be assertive, persistent, and strong believers in transformation. They should be patient and maintain vigor to achieve excellence, as the chase for quality is an unending journey.

There are numerous factors that help achieve substantial and sustained results from the quality initiatives of an organization, such as well-defined policies, a wide range of products and services, and a sustained and superlative customer service. Of course, there are other determinants too, such as empowered and engaged employees, peer involvement, and transparent and ethical business practices. However, in my experience, at the top of all these constituents lies the element of leadership.

Leadership is the cornerstone of excellence that can make or break companies. Without leadership commitment and support, most of the quality initiatives across the organizations either fail or continue without the same momentum and zeal with which they were embarked upon.

I wish to propose the following recommendations for new quality professionals:

- Believe in yourself and be a positive force in the organization.
- Believe in the power of hope, as hope keeps the quest for quality alive.
- Adapt to change. Change is the only permanent thing in life.
- Develop analytical and problem-solving skills. Develop the ability to interpret data and use statistical tools.
- Acquire proper communication skills. Effective communication sets a person apart from the crowd and helps to accomplish tasks quicker.
- Acquire planning and project management skills.
- Have the proper knowledge of quality standards and processes.
- Make it a habit to read at least one book on quality every six months.

Reference

Parasuraman, A. P., Zeithaml, V. A., and Berry, L. L. (1985). A Conceptual Model of Service Quality and its Implication for Future Research. *Journal of Marketing* 49, 41–50.

Chapter 4

High Performance through People

This chapter presents profiles of Nancy Nouaimeh and Raju Ravi Prakash. Both Nouaimeh and Prakash discuss their passion for quality and how, within their organizations, they develop people for quality. In the first part of this chapter, Prakash, who has twenty years of experience in managing quality at Khansaheb Civil Engineering LLC, explains the importance of people management for achieving quality performance in the organization. In the second part, Nouaimeh explains what it means to develop people for quality, citing her experience at Abela & Co. LLC. Both are wonderful quality professionals who provide us with their humble perspectives.

Profile 1: Raju Ravi Prakash, Khansaheb Civil Engineering LLC

Prakash is a group quality assurance (QA) manager who has primarily worked in the construction industry and has overseen the implementation of the ISO 9001 standard across several business units.

Introduction

I joined Khansaheb in 1996 when the turnover of the company was approximately 450 million UAE dirham. Now we have reached a turnover of approximately 1.2 billion UAE dirham. I attribute this success to putting in place a user-friendly system and effectively monitoring the performance of the process through measurable objectives at various functions and levels as a part of continual improvement. For many years, I have handled the implementation and maintenance of a quality management system in line with the requirements of the ISO 9001 standards. My interest in people management stems from over twenty years of working experience as a quality professional and expert with the ISO 9001 standards across the business. Khansaheb also encourages its employees to share their ideas about how to do things better in the following areas: (1) How can we encourage better communication with our teams? (2) How can we improve our tools, materials, or processes? (3) How can we better care for the environment? (4) How can we engage people for quality?

When I joined the organization, I could see that the majority of the staff had been with the company for more than fifteen years. Some of them definitely used old-school thinking, so it was quite a challenge to make the process owners understand the eight quality management principles we were to implement and their benefit on implementation. I had to hold one-on-one discussions with the project team members, and we formed a small quality team that in turn coordinated with the relevant team members. As we looked into customer/project requirements, we had to design relevant documents and use these documents on a trial basis for the creation of records. These records soon proved to be a very powerful tool in dealing with day-to-day activities with consultants and subcontractors. This exercise provided a solid platform for involving people at various levels. The end results yielded facts and figures, which meant the company had fewer customer complaints and obtained excellent customer satisfaction scores. In my opinion, the introduction of key performance indicators (KPIs) was another good initiative at the company. We saw drastic improvements, especially in the proper delivery of items in line with our quality policy.

I strongly believe that employees are the pillars of the organization. To me, people are the most important resource for any organization. I believe that quality management relies on the involvement of people for the success of all processes and strategies at various functions and levels. The best way to involve people in quality management systems is to take ownership and responsibility in order to resolve obstacles. Here are my observations for people success: First, you should actively seek out ways to make improvements and to improve competencies, knowledge, and experience. Second, you should share your knowledge and experience in groups; everyone in the group should have the right to share their knowledge skills and experience in the group. Doing so will allow the organization to strengthen the departments by ensuring that they are able to operate smoothly and correctly and in a professional manner. Each person who is involved will then start to focus on the formation of value for the customer, which will then allow for the promotion of the organization's goals. Innovation is a key part of fielding new workers to monitor and achieve the organization's objectives.

I have found that involvement makes people passionate and proud to be part of the organization. People at all levels are the essence of an organization, so their full involvement enables their objectives to be used for the organization's benefit. Figure 4.1 shows the plan-do-check-act (PDCA) process for people management.

I believe that quality is a mind-set, and I think that getting our employees to adopt a quality mind-set is the real key to producing high-quality products and services. The employees must feel a sense of ownership. That is, they must feel responsible for the outcome of anything connected with the product

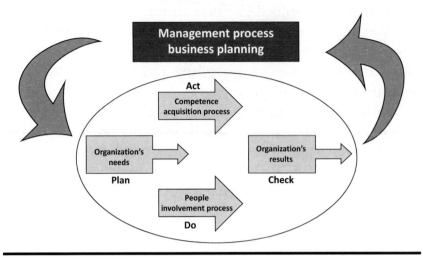

Figure 4.1 PDCA management process for business planning.

or service they work with. People always take better care of something they own compared with things they do not own. With ownership, employees will feel a sense of pride when hearing that their product or service has the highest reputation in the marketplace.

Teams are another important aspect of managing quality, although team-building is a huge process that takes time, training, and perseverance. Often, the entire culture of the workplace itself must go through some significant changes to be conducive to a teamwork philosophy. Special attention may be needed when building teams with employees from other cultures.

I have learned several other lessons for effective team management over the years. Input from all employees should be encouraged and expected at all times. Trust and good communication are essential. Team members must be able to communicate openly and freely and be able to rely on the information conveyed to achieve team objectives. When supervisors begin to seek employees' input and entrust them with key responsibilities, the employees will see this as a gesture of trust. By setting this example, supervisors will promote trust among the team members, who will then learn to reciprocate that trust.

Initiatives in Leveraging the People
Enabler within Khansaheb

Khansaheb has built a reputation within the construction industry of fostering excellence. This reputation is based on a number of initiatives established by the current group general manager with the active cooperation of the top management team. These initiatives are based on his determination to bring to life the Khansaheb vision of "redefining the future for people and places." This vision has been enshrined in our values: (1) Do the right thing. (2) Everyone has a voice. (3) Bring "better" to life. (4) Take pride in what you do.

The Khansaheb management believes that these values need to be translated into tangible, measurable actions that will show in the quality of work the company does. In an effort to establish best practices and proactive employee development, Khansaheb has instituted several systems and practices that help to improve the capabilities of its people. These include five initiatives: (1) a training center in Jebel Ali, (2) a middle managers program (MMP), (3) frontline supervisors training (FLST), (4) SustainAbilities, the company's sustainability program, and (5) rewards and recognition.

What Inspires Me to Be a Quality Management
Leader in My Firm and Industry?

For me, I am inspired by strong leadership qualities, where people show efficient time management and motivational skills and effective communication during the implementation of well-defined policies. I am inspired by people who face challenges during the delivery of their projects. I am not afraid of failure; I strongly believe that the word *fail* stands for "first attempt in learning."

My message to other quality professionals is, first of all, to keep one thing in mind: quality is everybody's business. Strictly follow the quality management principles. Thoroughly understand the requirements of the customer and deliver the product without compromising on quality. The maintenance of records using meaningful information is very important, as the objective evidence helps in sorting out many issues during the handling of projects.

My message to business leaders and CEOs is that everyone is important in an organization. The involvement of people using an open-minded approach is a healthy sign for any company's success. The introduction of rewards and recognition will bring fame and will motivate employees to do their best. Leaders must strongly discourage the blame culture.

As for my recommendations to new quality professionals on the skills they should develop, I think that the very first thing is to be empathetic—to have a positive attitude and an open-minded approach and, again, avoid a culture of blame. People should be involved in the problem-solving process by using tools such as fishbone (or cause-and-effect) diagrams. They must be in the habit of reading drawings and specifications thoroughly in order to understand the customer's requirements. This skill will help them to gain the confidence of consultants and their customers and will lead to having a professional approach. At any cost, companies should not compromise on quality with people, materials, machinery, and methods of execution.

Conclusion

Organizational success is purely based on people. Employees are the pillars of the organization. The delivery of projects on time and within budget by doing the job right the first time is one of the key milestones of organizational success. The training of employees adds value to the business; this brings in a professional approach, which is nothing but a combination of competence, confidence, and belief that will allow the company to obtain repeat orders. These factors will all lead to customer satisfaction. The customer is the king. Repeat orders can only be received if the delivery of the product is to the customer's satisfaction, by doing the job right the first time. As noted above, the key thing is to be empathetic and to have a positive attitude using an open-minded approach, rather than casting blame.

Profile 2: Nancy Nouaimeh, Abela and Co. LLC

Nouaimeh has worked in fields such as microbiology and food services management certification, and she has over thirteen years of experience, including ten spent exclusively in the UAE. She has extensive knowledge of quality methodologies such as total quality management (TQM) (master's level), Lean Six Sigma (green belt certified), the EFQM Business Excellence model, various ISO standards (22000, 9001, and 14001), OHSAS 18001 plus auditing, process mapping, and continuous improvement programs such as kaizen and 5S.

Introduction

I am usually known for being a serious and highly results-oriented person. Being the quality professional in my organization, where I am in charge of improving processes and ensuring the consistency of practices among chefs and operations teams, requires me to be strict, especially in the first few years after I started in my role. And because part of my job was to find areas for improvement and to dig deep to find the root cause of problems, I gained a reputation as the "tough quality lady," which was not much fun when people used the nickname to introduce me to people who had just joined the company. Eventually, that changed.

Two years ago, I worked with a food engineer trainee from France who spent six months in my department. One day, she made a remark that flipped the whole image I had of myself. She said, "You have the right personality and character for the job; you're made for it." What a relief that was! And the funny thing is that, in the end, I discovered that I was still taking my reputation of "tough quality lady" seriously, while everybody else had moved on and appreciated the improvements my department had achieved for the company.

In early 2016, I started a new class on quality in the workplace called the Gemba House of Quality, intended for junior chefs and food and beverage (F&B) staff to teach them about the Japanese concept of *gemba*. The challenge I faced was to make the class appealing to them, and both fun and motivational. We put a lot of effort into it. At the end of the first session, our CEO questioned a few of the attendees and asked them how tough the course was. To his surprise (and mine), the staff answered, "Tough? Not at all! We enjoyed it. We learned a lot. We didn't know quality could be fun and enjoyable."

So if a company wants to derive substantial and sustained results from its quality initiatives, the most important factor is to create a structure where the quality function presents a balance between decentralized and centralized activities. In many organizations, the quality department is often thought of as a policing agent whose role is to ensure that all standard procedures are followed, while in organizations, the burden of implementing quality standards and improvement initiatives falls only under the umbrella of the quality department. The success and sustainability of the quality drive, in both of these scenarios, is doomed to have a short lifespan.

The only way for quality to succeed in any organization is to have it integrated within the other functions and partially performed by each department, which in return will demonstrate self-sustained motivation and acquire skills to measure current performance, identify areas for improvement, and design improvement projects that will be best suited for the organization and its clients. In other cases, all departments follow the PDCA cycle or the DMAIC (Define, Measure, Analyze, Improve, and Control) methodology to continuously improve and sustain their results. The quality activities that can then be decentralized and shifted from the quality team to the other departments will then be primarily related to process improvement through programs such as kaizen, Lean, and Six Sigma. As they say, no one is better at identifying the points of difficulties and necessary improvements than those who are doing the job.

In this context or structure, a key role of quality is to be a learning agent, provide guidance, and monitor and align where gaps are identified—a function that remains centralized to ensure that all initiatives across the organization are appropriate, add value to the clients, and serve the organization's short- and long-term objectives. The empowerment and defined role of the quality department, in this case, needs to be well established by the top management of the organization, and correct boundaries should be drawn and made known to all to facilitate the quality work and to support the establishment of positive quality. Culture across the organization is another important item. Once roles are clearly set, with plans that align with the strategic objectives of the organization, regular reviews will determine the success of the initiatives and the sustainability of the results.

How Has Quality Helped My Company?

As of the summer of 2017, I have worked for ten years at the same company, which is a leader in food services management in the UAE. Back when I first joined the company, food safety was (and still is) the company's number-one priority, as it should be for any company in the food sector. The company was among the first in the country to be HACCP (Hazard Analysis Critical Control Point) certified. For some reason, the company had no quality department when I started. After six months of successful probation, I was assigned the task of establishing a full-fledged quality department, but it felt like my department would be competing with food safety to gain the attention of the people in the field/operations and production sectors.

I slowly started to build my department, focusing mainly on mapping processes, identifying performance measurements, standardizing procedures, establishing required standards and manuals, and enhancing consistency across over 120 locations. Over the span of the next four or five years, my work included projects for purchasing and stores, HR, operations, maintenance, and the culinary unit. After a few years, when we decided to certify the company according to an ISO standard, we chose ISO 22000:2005, the food safety management system (which has HACCP at its core). At the time, we had around 40 percent compliance with the management elements of ISO 9001:2008. After I was requested to lead the project, the challenge became even bigger, and I had to obtain the buy-in of all parties in the company in following my quality leadership for food safety certification. I started building on the success of the initiatives I had used so far, including many of the quality concepts and tools, and I used Dr. W. Edwards Deming's fourteen points for management, in addition to team-building activities, to break the barriers between the departments involved and to move forward with the project. It was all about modifying the culture and mindset and focusing on a key element to make a drastic change in the way work was done: measurement. That focus was very difficult to achieve in the creative environment in which the chefs worked.

The project started first with lengthy brainstorming sessions that were very much needed to establish clear accountability, align the team, and prepare a detailed project charter and timeline. We also had to embark on an intensive training program on the ISO standard requirements. After eight months of hard work, the system was ready for certification, but this only occurred because of the internal efforts of a well-tuned and cross-functional team from food safety, quality, purchasing, operations, and the culinary unit. Everyone talked the same language, focusing on reducing non-added-value activities and transforming our processes to match world-class catering companies.

In 2013, after we had been certified for two years, a third-party audit with one of the world's best certification bodies achieved a compliance score of 92 out of 100, which was the best in the UAE in our industry. The work of the ISO team is still ongoing, with regular meetings and more improvement projects every year, which has culminated in outstanding results, including

- Food Safety Excellence Culture Assessment (TSI-2015, score 81)
- Food Safety and Quality Excellence Culture Assessment (TSI-2016, score 82, grade A–, the highest in the industry group: quality 81.4, food safety 82.6)
- Improved supplier performance
- Reduced client complaints related to quality and food safety
- High grades in municipality inspections

Interestingly, one of the most important lessons I have learned from my career in quality, and from leading the quality department in a multicultural, multisite organization with a workforce of more than 3000 employees, is that the alignment of each department and employee is crucial to sustain any standard or system we have in place. Understanding the purpose of the quality initiatives—how they link together, interact, and integrate with the other systems in place—is a success factor, with an equal focus on *internal* and *external* customers, where the former are often overlooked. When we treat the internal users of our processes as customers—by looking at each of the touch points and identifying their requirements, added-value and non-added-value activities, and best practices to implement—only then can we be sure that the processes are being run efficiently.

In addition, because departments and their employees often by default focus on their own areas of work, they fail to commit (usually unintentionally) to the improvement projects that other departments call for. This likely occurs in the absence of a strong commitment from the leadership of the organization to quality, excellence, and continuous improvement. Because quality touches all areas of the business and their processes, a common understanding of the need for quality tools and a quality mind-set should be made evident for all. And, of course, the support from top management in providing the necessary resources for a strong training and learning program is a cornerstone of this idea.

One of the key focus areas of our food safety management system was to improve the communication and knowledge of food safety among junior and middle management staff to ensure their full involvement in implementing and maintaining the system. This area included the transfer of required knowledge from the food safety team to the management staff and to capture lessons learned from the field back to the team. Over two years, we implemented several projects to support the following:

- *Specific job duties matrix*: This matrix captures all specific assignments related to food communication, employee engagement, teamwork, and decision-making with facts and statistics. It uses the leadership, environment, strategy, safety, quality, process works, customer focus, continuous improvement, occupational health and safety (OHS), and operations of the key staff in each kitchen by providing an assigned and trained reliever and recording all the documentation needed to accomplish the work per the established standard.
- *Standards manuals*: We organized all necessary information for the operational staff in specific manuals (e.g., cleaning, emergency response, F&B best practices, and safe work instructions), including numerous illustrations to

be used as visual aids to facilitate the employees' understanding and to bypass any language barriers. We translated material into employees' native languages whenever
possible.

■ *Quality workshops*: We conducted special quality workshops in the kitchens through practical demonstrations.

■ *Lean waste identification posters and games*: Using examples from each and every operation, production area, and
department, we designed posters and created games with
junior staff to discuss all forms of waste.

■ *Recognition*: We used a scoring system to record positive
and negative observation points related to various teams'
safety practices, which improved the teams' scores and
provided motivation.

These all resulted in improved engagement in quality and
food safety and better decision-making, which improved the
company's level of safety. I personally find that, because each
of these methodologies or models should be applied differently and will yield different results and consequences in different contexts, but the basics always remain the same, I can't
say that one model or methodology is superior to the others.
In other words, based on what the organization intends to
achieve, it should choose the methodology that fits the organization's needs. The accuracy of the results and improvements
the company observes are conditional on the correctness and
thoroughness of the implementation or usage of the chosen
methodology.

I will elaborate more with a few examples. In my opinion,
certification to an ISO standard is a very efficient improvement
tool, especially when coupled with the implementation of
Lean programs, for example. But this certification is subject to
the competence of the implementation team in (1) balancing
and limiting the amount of documentation to what is necessary for the correct flow of information and data, (2) keeping
the system flexible without jeopardizing its integrity and the

consistency of practices, and (3) having an efficient review and updating process. Otherwise, systems like this are sometimes viewed as complex and tedious to manage. In our case, we were able to ensure 92 percent compliance, and this compliance was internally achieved by a cross-functional team from inside the organization, without the help of a consultant. If companies use off-the-shelf systems and do not adapt them to the needs of the organization, then they will risk having gaps in their systems, which will lead to limited improvements and a lack of positive impact from the certification of the processes.

The EFQM model, when followed and implemented in some UAE organizations, enables them to achieve gold in the Dubai Quality Award (DQA), while others barely earn DQA recognition. The model is the same: it is all in the implementation and the maturity of the approaches and their refinement; this requires having a strong review process in place, which people often do not realize.

What Inspires Me to Be a Quality Leader?

When I look at (1) the amount of time people waste on correcting defective work, (2) the lack of efficiency in achieving important tasks (which then directly affects the business and its clients' satisfaction), and (3) gaps in communication flows, especially key information, among many other negative practices, I can't help but feel proud and motivated to use my skills and knowledge of quality as a differentiator and change agent to make the organization where I work perform better, improve, and grow. This gives me great satisfaction to see that I can better things by transferring my knowledge in improving processes and results to other colleagues and departments, which, when coupled with their competence in their fields of expertise, results in improved efficiency.

Being a results-oriented person by nature, when I see the positive outcome of the improvement projects we implement, it inspires me to do more. Dr. W. Edwards Deming said, "Quality is everyone's responsibility," which motivates me to continuously work on maintaining the positive quality vibe in my organization, where everyone feels as engaged as the quality department does in ensuring that our clients receive the best-possible-quality products and services.

Conclusion

One of the most important lessons I have learned from my career in quality, and from leading the quality department in a global and multicultural organization with thousands of employees, is that the alignment of each department and employee is crucial to sustaining any standard or system. Understanding the purpose of the quality initiatives, and how they interact with other systems, leads to success. We focus on both internal and external customers, particularly because the former are often overlooked, which helps us to improve our efficiency. Departments and their employees often focus on their own areas of work and thus fail to commit to improvement projects, which often occurs because of a lack of managerial commitment to quality, excellence, and continuous improvement. Quality touches all areas of the business, so everyone should have a common understanding for the need for quality tools and mind-sets, and management should be committed at every step.

Our profession is extremely valuable to any business's growth and sustainability. While our roles may evolve significantly in the future, as the current research shows, the need for a quality mind-set to focus efforts on required improvements will grow even bigger in the future. Quality tools and methodologies will be useful in areas such as innovation and sustainability, where structured approaches and measurements are necessary to demonstrate the effectiveness of new ideas and to determine their impacts both before and after implementation. Quality professionals might see their functions changed to broader scopes; regardless of the sector and the titles given to quality professionals, their role will remain crucial in creating a culture of excellence in the organization, where all employees strive to give their best in terms of efficiency and productivity in order to help achieve better performance and to enhance the company's results and bottom line.

But this is not an easy task. The American Society for Quality (ASQ)'s 2016 "Global State of Quality" report (no. 2) reported the top five quality challenges as follows, which, in my opinion, are also representative of the situation in our region (although the percentages may vary) and will require further efforts to improve quality contributions.

■ Challenge 1 (39 percent of respondents): Quality competes for resources in the organization.
■ Challenge 2 (37 percent of respondents): Use of technology to ensure quality is uneven.
■ Challenge 3 (32 percent of respondents): Lack of uniform quality standards.
■ Challenge 4 (32 percent of respondents): Use of technology for metrics is uneven.
■ Challenge 5 (30 percent of respondents): Lack of specialized training for employees.

To gain the buy-in of their CEOs in providing the necessary resources and investing in the technology needed for quality, quality professionals need to start talking the language of CEOs and finance by demonstrating the positive business impact of quality. The frequent changes in the market related to quick shifts in consumer trends, the spread of social media, and increased online markets all present a challenge for companies that strive to keep their competitive advantage. These changes will also require them to develop new creative products and services promptly, in an agile and timely manner, to meet the new demands. Managing multicultural workforces with an increased proportion of millennials is yet another internal challenge for many companies. In the absence of a sound quality management system in such contexts, the risk of deviation from the company's established quality standards and objectives will become greater, which will then threaten the success of the company's current process delivery as well as the delivery of new projects.

The ASQ's 2016 research shows that among world-class organizations, 100 percent have invested in quality, trained all employees, and used technology to improve quality awareness; 96 percent see quality as a strategic and competitive differentiator; and 85 percent promote challenging quality goals to drive performance. It is more evident now than ever that quality is a strategic asset for world-class organizations and is a competitive differentiator. Hence, local companies that aim to design world-class processes to establish or sustain a competitive edge need to demonstrate a strong commitment from their leadership to increase the company's investment in quality and to make quality a part of the performance management of the company.

Chapter 5

Building a Culture of Continuous Improvement

This chapter presents profiles of Dr. Ramakrishna Akula and Mr. Amit Chana.

Profile 1: Dr. Ramakrishna Akula

Dr. Akula has expertise in integrated management systems, the European Foundation for Quality Management (EFQM) excellence model, Lean, and 5S, and has worked in the oil and gas engineering services, gas equipment research, LP gas bottling, and marketing industries over the past sixteen years of his career. He was a winner of the ASQ UAE Quality Professional Award in 2016. In this section, Dr. Akula explains the process approach he takes to improve quality.

Introduction

What inspires me to be a quality leader is my passion for excellence. I have implemented the RADAR (results, approach, deployment, assessment, and refinement) concept in developing automated loading sheets for special liquid gas products in road tankers for Emirates Gas. These principles have helped to attain zero human errors and have drastically reduced cycle times in precisely preparing loading sheets. Emirates Gas has an exclusive product called Emirates Gas Aerosol Propellant for perfume and spray applications. The product undergoes stringent quality norms and is loaded onto dedicated road tankers for delivery to customers. In order to achieve a specific blending of the product, engineers at Emirates Gas need to go through American Society for Testing and Materials (ASTM) tables and calculate the required blend based on ambient temperature and product storage tank temperature. This is a very time-consuming process (fifteen minutes per loading sheet), and any error in transferring data may lead to blending errors (the *results* part of RADAR). When demand increased, the engineers used to spend a lot of time preparing these loading sheets, and corrections had to be made several times due to minor errors in the field operations.

I decided to automate the process (*approach*) and developed an Excel-based system (*deployment*) for preparing the loading sheets. Now engineers only need to key in the ambient temperature, the tank temperature, and the required blend to prepare the sheet, and the automated system prepares the loading sheet in less than one minute (*assessment*). The users are very happy, as they no longer need to go through the cumbersome process, and the organization saves on time, which can be used for other productive work. Based on user feedback, the company's customer details and standard tankers are also incorporated into automated sheets for ease in preparation (*refinement*). Further, based on the results of the automated sheets, the system was extended to ISO-tanker loading for export shipments.

During the implementation process, I learned that most of the stakeholders were aware of the solution, but no one had taken the lead in integration. Communication and leadership helps in initiating quality improvement projects, but continuous commitment to quality helps to reach the ultimate goal.

How Have I Contributed to Improved Quality?

Emirates Gas selected the EFQM framework in order to provide consistent and sustainable quality deliverables to its customers. I have had a positive experience implementing the EFQM framework for processes at Emirates Gas. Our organization deals with hazardous and flammable products, which require higher safety norms, in addition to customer-specific requirements such as delivery preferences and specific product types, among other things. *Process focus* helps us to deliver on our promises to our customers in a safe and timely manner without incident.

Emirates Gas implemented the ISO quality system in 2006. Organizational processes are defined in the quality manual in the form of end-to-end process interaction mapping. These process interactions were reviewed and refined during the implementation of the EFQM framework in 2009. Over a period of time, several new processes were added due to increased product lines and expansion into various departments. Based on my experience, the top management's commitment is the most important thing to drive the process focus approach. In addition, system implementation will only be successful if all the people in the organization are involved and committed to quality deliverables.

Good process architecture in an organization can be developed by forming a team comprised of top management, subject matter experts, key operational and technical members, sales and marketing members, and safety committee members; end users and customers should be involved whenever possible. This kind of multidisciplinary team can map all processes after a thorough review. Once the processes are mapped, they should be subjected to review at frequent intervals or whenever changes in the process occur. These processes can also be subjected to process optimization tools such as using Lean management principles. In our organization, a small team comprised of multidisciplinary department members was formed to define the quality processes. These processes are subject to regular reviews by the Emirates Gas Lean committee for optimization. This approach has helped to capture a holistic view of processes from different perspectives (e.g., operations, safety, marketing, and customers) and accommodated various requirements from different departments and end users. The review in the Lean committee also identifies any bottlenecks in the processes and then streamlines them. Value stream mapping and Lean cases are useful in providing the basis for optimization. Several processes as well as the organization as a whole have benefited from this optimization in ways both tangible and intangible.

Every organization faces certain barriers in the implementation of such initiatives. The lack of top management drive is one such barrier. If the drive is not there from the top management, then the organization may not be in a position to define the processes at the initial stages. If the communication is not clear and transparent from top to bottom, then the organization may not receive the intended benefits from its employees. Similarly, if the multidisciplinary team members do not offer commitment, then the organization may face difficulties during the implementation stage due to unexpected process issues. In order to avoid these barriers, top management should define the team charter during the formation stage with clear roles, responsibilities, and accountability for each team member. The organization should also have defined policies to attain efficient review and refinement processes.

In any organization, employees at the lower levels (the general workers) are in the implementation stage. If the employees are clear on the processes and have defined processes, procedures, and work instructions, then the company can expect sustained quality output. But if there is no clarity in the approach, then quality output *may* be achieved, depending on the employees' skills and experience, but sustainability may not be achieved. Thus, the process focus is essential and fundamental to quality management in any organization.

Conclusion

New professionals should work in cross-functional depart-ments and projects and work toward understanding the overall processes of the organizations they serve. Having this kind of initiative helps new employees understand quality from differ-ent perspectives in order to design meaningful solutions for organizations in today's complex environment. Dedication and a commitment to quality are the most important requirements for quality professionals, and the continuous assessment and refinement of implemented processes helps to capture lessons for betterment. As role models, business leaders should focus on quality at the strategic level with a high level of commit-ment to and involvement in delivering the desired output. In my opinion, the EFQM model integrates every relevant aspect of any business for sustained results, and the model can easily be applied to any kind of organization. Overall, sustained com-mitment to quality is necessary to achieve outstanding results.

Profile 2: Amit Chana

Amit Chana has sixteen years of experience in diverse indus-tries including banking, retail, financial services, travel and hospitality, and supply chain operations. He has expertise in Six Sigma, Lean, COPC, PCMM, PRINCE2, ITIL, PMP, and eSCM, and he has been the recipient of the Malcolm Baldrige Quality Award and the CII-EXIM Quality Award.

Introduction

My inspiration to achieve quality stems from my desire to transform processes, departments, and the organization as a whole. Not many functions in any organization provide this kind of scope and opportunity. Quality projects are tools that can weave all of these things together so that you can take your organization forward. Truly, you should make quality part of your business strategy so that it becomes part of the culture. I strongly believe that the following are the most important factors in determining an organization's success in deriving substantial and sustained results from its quality initiatives: (1) management commitment, (2) the selection of the right initiatives and methodology, (3) the positioning of initiative in the organization, (4) the availability of appropriate resources and "fit for purpose" tools, (5) the engagement of employees across the organization, (6) making quality initiatives part of your business strategy and vision, (7) using capability building to drive quality initiatives by training employees across the organization, (8) having a robust reward and recognition program supported by a comprehensive communication plan, and (9) having strong governance and the frequent involvement of senior management.

My Experience with Six Sigma

I worked with Max New York Life Insurance in India as a quality leader, and we were able to implement quality initiatives across the organization, which covered the whole country, including over 2000 branches and over 10,000 employees. We also won a number of awards for our quality programs and innovations, which required a sustained effort from the central corporate team with unconditional support from the senior management team. Having management commitment and making quality a part of the business strategy were key. A business quality council was also created within the management and board levels.

We implemented Six Sigma in Max New York Life Insurance across the organization. In the early years, we observed that we were unable to get the positioning of the program right. We created a communication and R&R (reward and recognition) group, which did a lot of exhibitions, presentations, road shows, mailers, quizzes, and that kind of thing across the organization. In addition, we launched the POY (Project of the Year) Award, sponsored by management and the board. The winning project every year was offered a free, fully paid trip anywhere in the world for the entire project team. This change created a lot of buzz in the system, and a lot of employees signed up to be trained in Six Sigma to lead projects. Within two years, we had a portfolio of over 250 projects across the organization. Some of these projects gave us substantial savings—often in double-digit multiples of what we had initially invested. Our customer experience ranking improved drastically, and we moved into the top three insurance companies in India based on brand and customer experience surveys run by an external third-party organization. We maintained the momentum and won multiple awards for our projects and program.

Most importantly, I am reminded of a funny story. Once, my first boss explained to me using a demonstration why averages are misleading. He brought ice and hot water into the classroom and showed us that if you put one hand into a 0°C pail of ice water and the other hand into a bowl of 50°C water, then on average you can enjoy a fantastic mild 25°C hand bath. Six Sigma works on the same assumptions, which many times are not "fit for purpose"!

Chapter 6

Tools for Quality

This chapter presents a profile of Dr. Rassel Kasim, a quality expert based in the UAE. This chapter focuses on providing impetus for implementing quality in organizations as well as discussing the useful tools that can be deployed in the implementation of quality. Dr. Kasim speaks his mind from a practitioner's perspective.

Introduction

I believe that there is more than one perspective on quality. The narrow perspective considers quality a practice to increase customer satisfaction and reduce cost—in other words, take actions to increase profit. This approach focuses on customer retention by enhancing the customer experience and reaching their expectations, especially for repeat business. The wider perspective of quality considers the different groups and stakeholders by identifying their needs and expectations and providing the drivers to exceed those needs and expectations.

I believe in quality as a way of life. We can apply quality in our organizations as well as in our homes. We may consider quality principles in communicating with business stakeholders and with friends and family members. This is because quality is based on tools and techniques to identify needs and to assure and control the delivery of those needs.

Basic Quality Tools

Quality tools are undoubtedly essential, which will be very clear if we know that effective quality implementations involve the basic quality tools in 90 percent of cases. A good start is to talk about the seven basic quality tools, otherwise known as Ishikawa's Seven Basic Tools of Quality. The tools are called "basic" because people do not require advanced skills to use them; they are simple yet effective.

I am not going to explain the tools here, because they are fairly common; instead, I will share the sequence that makes the tools meaningful and helps practitioners to see the big picture. In most situations we use the check sheet to collect data related to different processes in the organization, then we analyze the data by selecting the most appropriate tool. Among the seven tools, we may go with a control chart, a histogram, or a scatter plot. Then we may use the cause-and-effect diagram to find the root causes of the problem. Finally, Pareto analysis is a good tool for prioritizing the causes (Figure 6.1).

New Quality Tools

In addition to the seven basic tools, numerous other quality tools focus more on the decision-making process. These new management tools were developed by the Japanese Society for Quality Control Technique Development. The seven new tools are described in the following sections.

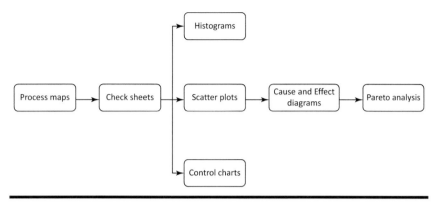

Figure 6.1   Logical map of the seven basic tools. (Based on Michael Brassard and Diane Ritter. 2004. *The Memory Jogger II*. Salem, NH: GOAL/QPC.)

Affinity Diagram

We usually use an affinity diagram, developed by the Japanese social scientist Jiro Kawakita in the 1960s, to take a quick look at the issues related to the problem we are examining. We do this by creating a number of themes and a hierarchy of ideas on a large surface. This diagram is used to discover the relationships between many ideas.

The affinity diagram can be used in many situations: for example, after we finish a brainstorming session and we want to look at all the ideas we have recorded. Or we may use it when we must reach a consensus between a group of people who are handling an uncategorized list of suggestions. The diagram can also be used to analyze the information we record while interviewing someone in a research project. The typical application of the affinity diagram, however, comes after creating a tree diagram. We apply this diagram using the following steps: first, record each idea on a card or board; second, search for relevant ideas; third, sort the cards into groups until all the cards are used; finally, once the cards are sorted into groups, classify large groups into subgroups to facilitate management and analysis. If you are doing the exercise in a team, using a whiteboard and markers is a good idea because the participants will be able to see it and read it from a distance. It is fine to have a few notes or ideas remain ungrouped; or, if you think one idea belongs to two different groups, then you may make a second card.

It is worth mentioning that after organizing the ideas into groups or themes, you might want to add a header to each group. The header is an idea that captures the crucial link among the ideas contained in the group of themes. In some cases, however, we may rephrase the header as a complete sentence to make the meaning clear. Sometimes it makes sense to create linkages between groups using lines, arrows, or circles. But the most important thing after you are finished drawing the affinity diagram is to put the diagram into practice and try to come up with recommendations.

Interrelationship Diagram

We may use this diagram to better understand the causal relationships between the different issues associated with one problem. It is also helpful to identify more issues while developing solutions to a problem. The interrelationship diagram urges team members to think in numerous ways instead of practicing one way of thinking. It is helpful for investigating the cause-and-effect connections among each of the issues, including the most disputable ones. In addition, the diagram enables key issues to arise normally, as opposed to being constrained by a dominant or powerful colleague. Finally, the diagram enables a group to distinguish one or more root causes, even when trustworthy information does not exist.

We usually follow certain steps to build the interrelationship diagram, which may be summarized as follows. First, we should have the issues related to the problem ready and defined before we start. We may use different tools, but the affinity diagram is a good one to use. Once the issues are identified, we write them on sticky notes (one issue per note) and post them on a whiteboard in columns. Each column should have the related issues grouped together. Second, we look at the issues one by one and check all the other issues that have caused or are affected by this issue, and then we draw a single-headed arrow from the cause issue to the affected issue. The team should repeat this activity until all the issues have been discussed. Third, we count the number of arrows that point to each issue on the board, and we write the numbers on the sticky notes. Fourth, we look for the notes with the most arrows attached to them, and we consider these to be the most important issues. The papers with the most outgoing arrows represent the root causes of the problem, while the papers with the most incoming arrows represent the performance measures. Finally, we highlight the key issues from the last step, and as a team we discuss the issues in detail and try to find ways to address them. It is common to find notes with many arrows attached to them, but they are not really key issues; in these cases, make sure to document the reasons why you excluded those notes.

Tree Diagram

The tree diagram is used to decide on the steps needed to address a certain problem; some practitioners say the tree diagram is similar to the work breakdown structure used in project management. From my personal experience, I may use a tree diagram to encourage employees and teams to think creatively while keeping their focus on the overall goals of the organization. These diagrams primarily rely on the use of graphic formats to simplify the analysis of set goals and to help manage complex scenarios.

The advantage of this tool has been proven in several areas, such as strategic and operational planning, and is especially useful for transforming the overall objectives into subgoals to make them clear and detailed. Tree diagrams can also be used to create systematic action plans and to present organizational goals graphically. Several sequential steps are involved in applying a tree diagram, which can be explained as follows:

1. First, ask yourselves: How can we achieve this goal?
2. Take advantage of the brainstorming method or any other techniques to generate ideas from participants on how to achieve the goal in question.
3. Write any ideas you receive in phrases, and make sure to begin each with a verb.
4. Discuss and refine the team's ideas. You may get new ideas at this point, and those can be added to the previous list of ideas.
5. Add the ideas to the tree diagram (separated and grouped) and name the main and sub-branches of the tree.
6. Review the overall outline to ensure completeness. To do this, you can ask the team questions at each stage, such as: "Have we missed something?" "Are all the activities we've added necessary?" "Will the implementation of these activities lead us to achieve our desired goal?"

In order to successfully apply the tree diagram, the team should review the logical links and the completeness of each level separately and make sure that the tree system is practical and applicable. The ideal tree diagram, if read from left to right, should provide the answer to the question, "How did we accomplish the goal?" If read from right to left, it should provide an answer to the question, "Why did we do all these activities?"

It is useful to take a range of actions after drawing a tree diagram, such as (1) choosing the best-documented ideas; (2) adding detailed information for each branch of the tree, such as the target, the resources required, and completion dates, among others; and (3) presenting the diagram to senior management and gaining their approval.

Prioritization Grid

When we have multiple alternatives and several criteria, prioritization grids can help us to make our decisions without engaging in complicated analyses. Using this tool is ideal in several situations. First, when the subject is critical for the company, the wrong decision may have serious implications, such as when selecting production technology or setting strategic initiatives. Second, if we want to use different criteria to make our decisions, and if some of these criteria are subjective, then using a prioritization grid can be helpful. Third, such grids can be useful when we want to select one option from a list of options.

We should keep in mind that because the prioritization grid is a time-consuming tool compared with other tools, we should make sure that participants are ready to spend time discussing and evaluating the options. It is good to mention that this tool can be applied with different stakeholders (e.g., customers) when we invite them to evaluate our services or their experiences with our organization.

Prioritization grids come in several different styles, which should be chosen based on the situation. I will explain the analytical criteria method, which I advise using in special situations such as when the team members must reach a consensus. If the participants disagree on the priority and importance of the evaluation criteria, then in some cases, a few of the participants might have a hidden agenda or personal interests, in which case it is also wise to use this tool. The following steps can be followed to apply a prioritization grid.

Criteria Weighting

(1) Make sure all the participants understand the topic under discussion and agree on what to be decided. (2) Draw a matrix with an equal number of columns and rows and list the agreed criteria to be followed when making the decision

as column headings and repeat them as row headings; then, shade the diagonal cells in the matrix that share the same labels. (3) Compare each criterion in the row labels to each criterion in the column labels (i.e., pair-wise comparison). Decide which one is more important using the following scale: 1=both are equal, 5=row is more important, 10=row is extremely important, –5=row is less important, –10=row is extremely unimportant. (6) Add the inverse of the score you decided in the cell diagonally opposite inside the matrix. (7) Calculate the total rating for each row, and then add the row totals to find the grand total. (8) Divide each row by the grand total and write the answers in an additional column and label them as relative weights of the criteria.

Rating Options Against Criteria

(1) Create a new matrix, similar to the first one, and title it with the name of the first criterion. (2) List the options/alternatives you have as rows and column headings. (3) Repeat the same comparisons (pair-wise) using the same scale and same calculations, but between the options/alternatives and not between the criteria. (4) Make a new table for each criterion you have.

Summary Matrix

(1) Create a new matrix and add options as row labels and criteria as column labels. (2) In the column headings, add to each criterion its relative weight, as listed in the first table you made (criteria weighting). (3) In the first column, multiply the option weights from the first criterion matrix with the relative weight of the criterion you added to the label in the last step and write down the answer. (4) Repeat the same action for all columns. (5) Add the results across each row; this is the option score. The largest number represents the best choice.

Matrix Diagram

This diagram can be used for a variety of purposes. We may consider it a brainstorming tool to show the relationships between sets of issues or ideas, or to gain information on the strengths of a relationship, or about the role played by various members. Practically speaking, we can use the matrix diagram in different work situations. For example, if we (1) have more than one problem and want to segregate the problems and know which ones are affecting exact parts of the process, (2) want to consider customer needs and requirements and link them to work processes, (3) need to identify the cause-and-effect associations between issues, (4) sort out conflicts or overlaps between two projects or plans that will be implemented at the same time, or (5) form a team or task group and want to assign each member certain responsibilities.

The matrix diagram can be used in up to four dimensions, and we have six types to choose from: (1) the *L shape*, which links one set of items to itself or two sets of items to each other; (2) the *T shape*, which links three sets of items (set 1 with set 2, and set 2 with set 3, but not set 1 with set 3); (3) the *Y shape*, which links three sets of items (set 1 with set 2, set 2 with set 3, and set 1 with set 3); (4) the *C shape*, which links three sets of items together at the same time; (5) the *X shape*, which links four sets of items (set 1 with set 2, set 2 with set 3, and set 3 with set 4, but not set 1 with set 3 or set 2 with set 4); and (6) the *roof shape*, which links one set of items to itself only.

We usually use symbols to describe the relationships between items. The most common symbols describe the strength of the relationship between two items: we may use a double-line circle to indicate a strong relationship, a single-line circle for a moderate relationship, and a triangle to indicate potential or weak relationships. We may design and define our own symbols when we apply the matrix diagram to match the topic of discussion. Whatever the type we use, we follow general steps to develop the matrix, which are as follows: (1) agree what sets of items to compare; (2) select the most suitable matrix type; (3) draw an empty matrix; (4) add the items of each group to the matrix, either as column or row labels; (5) decide on the symbols you will use and describe them in legends; (6) do an item-by-item comparison and add the appropriate symbol to the cell at the intersection of the paired items; (7) analyze the output and try to discover any patterns.

Process Decision Program Chart

These charts are used to brainstorm possible problems or emergencies associated with the implementation of plans, programs, or enhancements. The team members often develop actions to prevent the expected problems. We have two options when using this diagram: either to update the plan to avoid the problems or to prepare solid responses in case the problems have already happened.

We always advise people to use the process decision program chart if the price of failure is too high, or if we have time constraints and delay is not an option, or if we have developed a complex plan with many details and sub-plans. In these cases, we use this tool to test the plan before we start implementing it. Most often, we apply the following steps when using this tool.

First, to use the decision diagram, we should do some preparation work, mainly by identifying the major goals and objectives of the plan, in addition to the main activities and the major tasks necessary to accomplish those activities. A tree diagram is the tool that allows us to organize our work and to prepare well; in the tree diagram, tasks will be presented as level 3, while main activities are level 2. Second, we start by looking at each task in the tree diagram; we discuss the task and brainstorm what could go wrong with it. Third, we highlight the most significant problems, and we add those problems as a new level (level 4) under the problems' related tasks.

Fourth, we set countermeasures for each expected problem from level 4, and we list them as level 5; these countermeasures might be changes to the original plan or responses to the problem (if it happened). Fifth, the team members evaluate each countermeasure and decide whether it is a good action or an impractical one; based on the nature of the plan we are dealing with, we may set criteria to assess the suggested countermeasures, such as time, cost, or complexity. Finally, the practical countermeasures are usually marked with an *O*, and the unpractical ones are marked with an *X*.

Activity Network Diagram

Also known as critical path diagrams or PERT diagrams, these diagrams are used for controlling projects, and they have the longest path in time from beginning to end. The diagram, which was developed in the United States in the 1950s, helps to set timelines for implementing projects and allocating resources appropriately. The main advantages of using an activity network diagram include (1) representing the project in a diagram that shows all activities and shows their association with each other, (2) forecasting the project's completion date and time, and (3) distinguishing between critical and non-critical tasks in the project (this allows for transferring resources from non-critical to critical tasks, which may reduce the project duration without increasing the budget).

The activity network diagram involves sequential steps, which are as follows:

1. Identify all project activities and organize them as a list.
2. Analyze each task or activity in relation to the other activities of the project in terms of the possibility of achieving the task alone or in parallel with other activities; it is a good idea to create a table that shows project activities and how they are linked to each other.

3. Represent the tasks on a network diagram, which should be drawn so that the activities are added at the network nodes.
4. Estimate the time required to complete each activity alone; the time to complete each task is estimated based on past experience or by logical intuition. The duration of some activities is easy to predict, although other activities are more complex and hard to be predicted.
5. Define the critical path using the network diagram. The critical path is the longest path in time from beginning to end; a delay in any of the critical path activities will cause a project delay.

It is good practice to update the network diagram periodically during project implementation. We usually record the real time for each activity, and in the meantime a new critical path may emerge. The critical path passes through the first point and the last point in the project. It is a continuous line, not a dotted one. The activities in the critical path are also divided into two types. The first is the actual or real activities, which are specific and time-bound achievements that require physical and human resources and are expressed in the network diagram in a normal line. The "dummy" activities are those that do not take time and do not require any resources to be implemented. The time taken is zero and is expressed on the network diagram with dotted lines.

One of the best ways to use the seven new tools is to consider them in a cycle of activities, where each tool provides inputs to another tool. One possible arrangement is shown in Figure 6.2.

Perception of Quality Tools

The current changes we are living through, especially the fourth revolution and quality 4.0, have had an impact on the usage of quality tools. This impact may be illustrated in the shift of perception among quality experts. A study based on a global survey in which fifty executives and quality experts

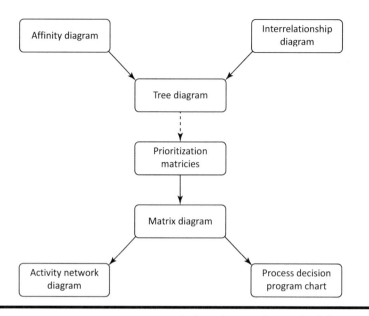

Figure 6.2   Seven management and planning tools: Typical flow source. (Based on Michael Brassard and Diane Ritter. 2004. *The Memory Jogger II*. Salem, NH: GOAL/QPC.)

were questioned revealed that 42 percent of respondents thought the effectiveness of the quality methods was decreasing, and 50 percent thought quality issues related to customers would increase in the next ten years. Practitioners in the UAE share a similar view. In a 2017 survey, one of the questions was whether the seven basic quality tools would stay effective. The results showed that three tools will most likely be outdated: check sheets, histograms, and Pareto charts.

Conclusion

Quality experts must respond to the current changes. The most effective way in my opinion is to increase our skills ourselves. The following skills are highly recommended:

■ *Big-data analytical skills*: Relying fully on statistics is no longer a practical option. Quality experts should acquire the basic skills to understand and analyze big data, both structured and unstructured, and to do their best to move from the hindsight stage to the foresight stage of data analysis, where value and efficiency is increased.

■ *Risk management skills*: These skills include identification, assessment, controlling, and monitoring emerging risks.
■ *User experience design skills*: These skills include all aspects of interactions between end users and the business; they are mainly about creating or developing services that will provide meaningful and personally relevant experiences to customers. This is coherently linked to the concept of design thinking.
■ *Process design skills*: These skills should remain essential in the future; well-designed processes will still be required because the automation of inefficient processes will only add more risk to the company.

Reference

Brassard, M and Ritter, D. (2004). *The Memory Jogger II*. Salem, NII.GOAL/QPC).

Chapter 7

Quality Awards and Certification: An Exceptional Journey

This chapter presents the profiles of quality experts in the UAE who hold key positions as quality award custodians, quality experts, and quality consultants. These experts have initiated several good practices over the last two decades and have coached a number of organizations in achieving excellence. The prominent personalities included in this chapter are Ms. Shaikha Ahmad Al Bishri, and Ms. Seema Sequeira, the director of the Business Excellence Award and a quality specialist, respectively, at Dubai Economy. Quality consultants Dr. Franco Pieracci and Dr. Laura Salasco also discuss their experience in quality implementation within UAE organizations.

Profile 1: Shaikha Ahmad Al Bishri and Seema Sequeira

As director of the Business Excellence department at Dubai Economy, I am responsible for various programs and initiatives, including the Dubai Quality Award, the Dubai Human Development Award, and the Dubai Service Excellence Scheme, all of which aim to promote quality, excellence, and best practices in doing business.

Today, the Business Excellence Awards are acknowledged both regionally and globally as a reliable benchmark for quality HR development and service excellence. Throughout their historic journey, the Business Excellence Awards have continued to enjoy the patronage and support of His Highness Sheikh Mohammed Bin Rashid Al Maktoum, vice president and prime minister of the UAE and ruler of Dubai. More than being recognized as a symbol of quality and excellence, these awards are a critical component of the past, present, and future of the UAE. Four years ago, Sheikh Mohammed launched his vision to transform Dubai into a smart city and to make the emirate one of the most technologically advanced cities in the world.

Dubai has deployed various initiatives and projects to achieve Sheikh Mohammed's vision and to transform the whole emirate—and not just any one specific industry—into a smart city. The Department of Economic Development (DED) in Dubai, for its part, has developed a strategy to harness the ongoing digital transformation of Dubai and to further boost economic growth, productivity, and global competitiveness. The DED sees the awards as an integral part of the ongoing efforts to enhance quality and business excellence across the emirate, in line with the goals to become a smart city. I am passionate about organizational improvement programs, particularly those focused on employee satisfaction and overall customer happiness.

I believe in creating a culture of quality and excellence. Today, the DED is constantly developing new standards for the Business Excellence Awards to promote competition among businesses and organizations across various fields and vital sectors. The next phase of the awards will see many qualitative developments and additions, which will further make it important for businesses to participate in and win the awards.

Seema Sequeira has supported the Dubai Quality Awards for the past twenty-three years and has been actively involved in carrying out quality, HR, and marketing initiatives from its infancy through development and successful implementation.

Profile 2: Dr. Laura Salasco: Perspectives from a Quality Consultant

As a consultant and temporary quality manager of companies from SMEs to multinationals, I have worked in over ninety organizations in the manufacturing field, including plastic, rubber, and metal; car design and manufacturing; and the design and manufacturing of electronic and electromechanical components. I also have experience in service organizations, including hospitality and health care, among others. I would say that I started my experience as a quality professional after attaining my quality management master's degree—one of the first of its kind—in 1992 in Pisa, Italy, the same city in which I had earned a degree in chemical engineering in 1987.

During my carrier as a quality professional, I have used and implemented many tools and methodologies, including (1) quality control statistical tools for product and process control, measurement, and the enhancement of process performance and capabilities (including X-R charts, Cp, Cpk, and DOE, among others); (2) the quality assurance methodologies used in the automotive sector, such as Quality Function Deployment (QFD), failure mode effectiveness analysis (FMEA), P; and (3) the quality management methodologies found in Six Sigma.

Simply put, the most important factor for success is the drive and sponsorship of top management. When that happens, top management can easily attain buy-in from the entire management, who will consequently involve all employees and workers.

When I was requested to work on an improvement project, the client (a casting house) was experiencing quality problems with their products, which were having a dramatic impact on the bottom line. The main issues seemed to be the client's existing non-compliant management processes and their competencies in problem-solving.

I reengineered their non-compliant processes and corrective/preventive action management processes, and I taught them the most common problem-solving techniques. I used the practical approach (by applying things directly to the problem during ad hoc workshops) instead of a theoretical approach. Although this was unexpected at the start of the project, I also had to add some staff behavioral and interpersonal communication coaching to reach the final outcomes: about a 50 percent drop in customer rejects and a 15 percent productivity improvement, which became the new organizational and sector benchmark.

I learned that when top management looks at certifications (e.g., ISO) or awards (e.g., the European Foundation for Quality Management [EFQM] Award, the Dubai Quality Award [DQA], Sheikh Khalifa Excellence Award [SKEA], and Mohammed Bin Rashid Al Maktoum [MRM] Award) only for marketing or recognition reasons, any designed and implemented improvement will not be sustainable, and the company will not consistently perform. In my experience, I learned that my greatest successes had originated in using a multi-methodology approach, supported by good emotional intelligence. By this I mean: first provide the organization with what they have asked for, then understand how to make it work and how to improve it. Most of the time, clients call an expert because they don't have the time or the competency to fix a situation. But before starting a project, it is not easy to have all the details; and the smallest ones can be the key.

Some years ago I had a client for ISO 9001 certification who decided not to calibrate a micrometer (an instrument that is used in quality control). I advised him that this could be a

problem during the certification process, because if the external auditor were to uncover the fact that an instrument that
is systematically used in quality control was not calibrated,
this would be a major non-conformity, and the certification
process would have to be stopped. He promised that the
external auditor would never discover this. Of course, during the audit, the auditor asked the quality control inspector
how he would control some technical characteristic. And, of
course, the inspector answered, "With this!" And he showed
him the instrument that the clients had said would never be
discovered!

Finally, for me, being in charge of quality management
means improving the quality of the products, services, and
processes of my organization, and to help my colleagues—all
of them, not just those in my department—do the same.

Finally, in my experience, quality principles are corre-
lated and contribute to the success of improvement projects. I
remember an experience with an OEM and POS printer manufacturer where, after sales assistance was not properly managed, their customers complained about delays in fixing and
repairing the product (which was actually a standard time for
repairs). The customers' complaints needed to be managed,
which further worsened the process.

The finding of the analysis was a result of teamwork.
Improvements in after-sales assistance were conducted with a
full focus on customer needs and expectations. After the new
process was implemented, the company communicated a standard time for reparation to all the customers. Of course, the
new process was a clear example of the continuous improvement and implementation of the organizational strategy. The
project produced a 75 percent decrease in customer waiting
times and actually transformed an area that needed improvement into a competitive advantage for the organization.

Finally, I think that emotional intelligence and humil-
ity are very important. When new quality professionals start
their careers, they will discover in their organizations many

"strange" implemented solutions that—based on their competencies—have to be different. Instead of presenting their new solutions, new quality professionals first need to understand the problem that the "strange" solution has previously addressed and solved. Only then should they ensure buy-in from the relevant stakeholders and finally provide a better solution.

Profile 3: Dr. Laura Salso: Learning from a Quality Consultant

In my twenty-two years of experience, the most important factor that determines an organization's success in deriving substantial and sustained results from its quality initiatives is the belief and commitment of the leadership of the organization. During my tenure at EFQM, I have been involved with some of the most advanced organizations in Europe. One example is of a global automotive manufacturer that achieved results such as a 16 percent productivity increase and a 25 percent carbon emission reduction over five years (this is an amazing result, considering that the baseline was already excellent), plus people's satisfaction and trust in leadership at the 99 percent level as a result of using the EFQM model. Another example is a health-care organization that achieved a 40 percent reduction in patient complaints, a 28 percent reduction in complaint response times, and waiting times far below the national average. They achieved these results through the commitment of top management, the involvement of the employees, and the use of the EFQM model as a strategic driver of performance improvement.

I strongly believe that quality improvement is decided and sponsored by top management, facilitated by the quality professionals, and carried out by the organization's employees (at all levels). Therefore, ambitious results can only be achieved if the people in the organization are as committed and passionate about improvement as the leadership and the quality professionals are. This requires knowledge and training, but more importantly communication, involvement, and engagement.

The EFQM model for business excellence is superior to any other methodology because it is a strategic (rather than tactical) driver of performance improvement. The EFQM model is a business model rather than a quality improvement model. It addresses all the components of an organization (i.e., all processes and/or functions). Furthermore, any organizational initiative or improvement tool can be categorized according to one of the nine criteria of the EFQM model, thus enabling the organization to rationalize all initiatives and improvements under one coherent approach. As a business excellence expert, I have benefited greatly from experiences in other organizational functions, such as product development or operations. This experience has supported my career progression in the corporate world and has also enriched my professional background and experience as a quality/business excellence professional and consultant. If possible, I suggest that quality professionals should try to gain experience in other functions, through lateral moves or secondary opportunities.

My message for business leaders in both public and private enterprises is to adopt the EFQM model as the strategic driver of performance improvement in their organization. If they are not familiar with the EFQM model, they can contact some of the experts in the field or (even better) connect with other leaders who have achieved outstanding results for their organizations thanks to the EFQM model.

In the UAE, implementation of the EFQM model is promoted by the highest levels of government through the endorsement of local excellence awards, such as SKEA, DQA, and the Sharjah Top Business Award, among others.

I am inspired by the world-class organizations I have had the privilege of working with and consulting for. Through the adoption and implementation of the business excellence principles, their leaders and employees have created winning environments and inclusive cultures, which then provide opportunities to thrive for individuals and teams alike. At one stage in my career, I was responsible for quality in a group of units that were undergoing reorganization. I had two key tasks: (1) transfer the policies and processes related to a specific activity from units that were being closed to other units in the group, and (2) manage the relations with the customers that were being transferred from the services of the closed units to the services of the new units. For both tasks, the challenging organizational context required appropriate stakeholder communications: the decisions of the corporate center needed to be conveyed with empathy and with appropriate detail regarding current and future plans, so that all stakeholders would be motivated to collaborate. At the same time, a systematic change management approach was required in order to ensure that all processes and specifications were transferred without errors or defects. This approach included the punctual monitoring of performance indicators before, during, and after the transformation exercise.

I would recommend that new quality professionals become involved in EFQM assessment as soon as their level of professional experience and their work schedule allow it. In the UAE, a first point of entry consists of applying to be an assessor in one of the local business excellence awards, such as DQA and SKEA, among others. The award offices provide the required assessor training and subsequent experience. It is also possible to apply for official EFQM assessor training.

The assessment experience provides great exposure to the excellence principles and also to the structures and working methods of other organizational functions, which is in line with my suggestion from above of seeking experiences outside the quality function.

Chapter 8

Towards Building a Culture of Business Excellence

This chapter presents a profile of Mr. Krishna Kumar, general manager of quality and business excellence for the Oasis Investment Company LLC/Al Shirawi Group. Mr. Kumar is a passionate quality leader who is ambitious about driving his organization toward excellence. He discusses his experiences with driving quality in his organization and shares valuable knowledge about using quality standards to achieve operational excellence.

Introduction

As a general manager of quality and business excellence, I have led quality efforts to implement ISO standards across all our group companies. I am passionate about each of these implementations, and I recognize the immense benefits that such systems bring to the organizations. In fact, if you need to see how these quality tools are used to drive organizational performance and the impact of those tools, you must visit our site; we would be happy to show you how they work for us. We are proud to be among those who have already begun to incorporate risk assessment and risk frameworks within the organization.

What Factors Are Important to Implement Quality Standards Successfully?

I really think there is a need for every manager to support participation in quality standards implementation. Truly, leadership plays a vital role in engaging all the stakeholders, since the leaders are the driving force of any such initiatives. They need to ensure the availability of required resources, and they also have to be accountable for guaranteeing the effectiveness of the implementation of business best practices to meet the necessary criteria and to qualify for and win the National Quality Award. These things will become possible by setting up the right objectives (and without forgetting to chase those goals), building an effective strategy with proper resource planning by assigning roles and responsibilities, communicating the same to all stakeholders, and leading the alignment of the National Quality Award criteria to the organization's business processes. The top management also needs to introduce a performance management program to the project, which will in turn lead to business improvement initiatives.

"What's in it for us?" is often the first question for every business. Rewards and recognition—which grab center stage for a good reason—definitely motivate everyone in the business. Goodwill and credibility, including a media presence, will help the business to have more mileage. Participation in the award program should not be made mandatory at any stage, as this needs to be practiced by an organization that has the right intentions and will pursue these goals without having to force people. Most businesses will want to chase tangible benefits rather than achieve technical efficiency and effectiveness; hence, the leadership's promotion and communication of the real business benefits will help the initiative to achieve better acceptance.

Middle management should act when top management shows its positive intent to deploy the quality criteria set for the award program. This will be done most effectively when the criteria are injected into the key business processes, as desired by the top management. Middle management carries the responsibility of deploying the program throughout the organization according to the project roles and responsibilities they have accepted from the leadership team. They drive the project by motivating and guiding the rest of the workforce below the line by letting them know why everyone in the company has to be a part of the process and what the positive and negative impacts will be when they decide to act on the roles and responsibilities assigned to them.

Training programs are the foundation of implementing the project and will also act as a method to achieve the set of competencies, both behavioral and technical. A training plan needs to be created with effective monitoring mechanisms for the objectives set for each session. This will ensure the effectiveness of the planning, execution, assessment, and improvement phases of the project. The sessions could be on awareness, documentation, implementation methodology, assessment methods, and improvement programs. These sessions will ensure the engagement of the stakeholders and hence will be one of the key deciding factors in the success (or failure) of the award program. Companies can also adopt quizzes, campaigns, and surveys that utilize the technology platforms. The key purpose these activities serve is to let the stakeholders know why they have to be a part of the process, what their roles are, how their contributions will be a deciding factor for the program, and what the benefits of the successful implementation of the ongoing project will be.

Communication and awareness among the employees is important to enhance their participation; in addition, benchmarking should be done for the other international global quality awards, and comparisons should be made to mature business practices that have been awarded by comparing the results from previous years. Case studies of the winning habits should be built and shared, lessons learned from any failures should be recorded and captured, and a points system with attractive government financial benefits for winning businesses should be introduced.

Audits play a very important role in measuring the effectiveness of the entire project. Audits will show the actual status of the project plan and the plan's execution status (planned vs. actual) against the same. The audits should focus on the high-impact areas of the project and should be conducted at regular intervals. The top management should also ensure that the audits are conducted by competent professionals using the right tools and available technology. This *check* process will guarantee the consistency of the project deployment by measuring the performance and compliance criteria established by relevant stakeholders (management and the authorities). This process also shows the status of the satisfaction levels of the stakeholders at all levels. Action plans and further reviews can be set using all these audit findings, which will lead to the improvement initiatives of the project. The success of the project deployment completely depends on the active engagement and commitment of the employees at all levels of the organization. This engagement will enable the key processes and technology platforms that have been brought in for the success of the project and the business.

The execution of the entire project plan completely depends on the active participation of all employees, which is only possible when they are committed and passionate about the project goals the leadership team has set.

What Are Our Best Practices?

The Oasis Investment Company, the holding company of the Al Shirawi Group, was founded in 1971 on the basis of a pure passion for business. Our founders, Abdullah Al Shirawi and Mohan Valrani, have embedded a sense of pragmatism into the culture of the group since the beginning. It is this pragmatism that has not only seen us through the most difficult of times but has also allowed us to capitalize on opportunities during favorable times. Our journey from a trading house to an industrial complex, and then on to a conglomerate comprised of trading, industrial, distribution, contracting, and service sectors, has seen its fair share of trials and tribulations, but we can honestly say that today, our employees (over 10,000) are richer in experience than their counterparts. A conglomerate of thirty-four companies, our operations span across the Gulf Cooperation Council (GCC) nations and have an exceptional track record in performance in almost all segments of operation.

The foundation for all our companies has been cast in the UAE, but today all our companies look at the world as their marketplace. In this age of globalization, we continue to grow at a steady pace. Speed is a virtue that we stand by at all times. The successful induction of our next generation into the business has allowed us to retain the advantages of remaining a family concern but at the same time has enabled us to act with speed in the hiring of top-grade professionals. Our group has been built on the premise of sheer hard work. We have progressed this far by believing in our values and by never shying away from putting in the effort needed to grow any business. For us, the journey has been a long one, but we see it as just the beginning of bigger things to come. Our next generation is now fully equipped to take the group forward to unimaginable heights. Krishna says that we want everyone who deals with us to see, understand, and experience that we provide high-quality solutions—and to reap the full benefits of working with a company where innovation, unrivalled quality, and the pursuit of excellence are day-to-day realities.

Al Shirawi Engineering Services has a meticulous way of setting strategic objectives. Every quarter of the financial year, the company conducts a strategy review meeting to understand the current strengths and weaknesses in the management (internal) and the socio-economic challenges prevailing in the market that need to be addressed for better performance (external). Through this opportunities and threats review, the company identifies the value stream for future growth. The technique to identify the areas of concern and opportunities is selected carefully, and workshop sessions are held by the CEO in an informal manner to encourage the top management team to air their views on the various challenges and opportunities.

With the adoption of the ISO 9001:2015 standards, a fundamental risk-based thinking methodology is being inculcated while the company reviews any business proposals or opportunities. All business risks are identified in advance through risks and opportunities probing sessions with the top management team. Risk mitigation is then undertaken to make the risks acceptable using controls. Detailed risks and opportunities registers are created that will undergo periodic scrutiny under the following circumstances:

■ Changes in the previously agreed scope.
■ Risks/opportunities due to changes in legal and legislative requirements.
■ Risks/opportunities due to diversification of resources, time, and cost.
■ Risks/opportunities due to volatilities in the market.

Al Shirawi Engineering Services understands the requirements of sustainability in the region. With that objective in mind, the company has created a sustainability initiative committee under the supervision of the CEO. The committee works for sustainable initiatives that are relevant for safeguarding the most important natural resources (e.g., electricity and water) and to reduce the company's carbon footprint. These matters have been taken care of by the following initiatives that have been conducted at the group level.

- Changing the traditional refrigerant-operated HVAC equipment with environmentally friendly R410A Energy Star–certified units, which enabled energy savings of 12–15 percent.
- Changing the traditional fluorescent lamps to LED lamps, which resulted in 22 percent reductions in per-unit consumption.
- Implementing a carbon footprint reduction campaign and reducing paper consumption by embracing technology in all activities, such as gaining approval through online portals and the attachment of documents in the company's ERP portal for vendor registration and management, all of which resulted in a 50 percent reduction in paper consumption.
- Installing waterless urinals, which resulted in massive water savings (a 38 percent drop in consumption).

Chapter 9

What and Why of Benchmarking

This chapter presents a profile of Ms. Indu Singhal. Talking about the most important factor that determines an organization's success in deriving substantial and sustained results from its quality initiatives, Ms. Singhal speaks about her experiences and highlights the role of benchmarking in achieving excellence in organizations. The chapter presents benchmarking best practices and specifically discusses the UAE experience with benchmarking.

Introduction

A focused leadership team empowered with the right human capital management initiatives is key to the successful implementation of quality initiatives. A balanced scorecard (BSC) may prove to be an effective tool for driving this strategy. Using human capital to drive processes to the optimum will undoubtedly result in an optimized customer experience. But clarity from the leadership team is what is most needed. With clarity, steering the organization toward success will be easy to do using a set of systematic frameworks. Governance procedures may be implemented using the BSC while also addressing risk. To make a BSC work, rational targets need to be set. These may be set using various inputs such as past performance, current macro-level organizational goals, available resources, market conditions, and, among other factors, benchmarking. Benchmarking one's own performance against that of another better performer is key to ongoing improvement. Benchmarking may be done within the region or within the industry. It may not always be against the competition. Benchmarking needs to be understood for what it truly represents. While numbers contribute toward achieving quantifiable comparisons, benchmarking need not be limited to numbers. The benchmarking of processes and initiatives is equally, if not more, important.

Dubai embraced this fact in 2015 by partnering with Emirates Business Management (EBM) International Consultants to launch the EBM Benchmarking Partners (EBM-BP) program, which has gone on to benefit scores of companies in the region. This program is a platform that has transparently brought together leading organizations to actively share data that they had previously held close. This program enables organizations to bring together their best practices on a common platform in a controlled environment via the EBM Benchmarking Club sessions that are conducted every month. Participating organizations demonstrate their key initiatives and learn from each other. Further, the EBM benchmarking visits take participants to the *gemba* of host organizations to learn best practices through live demonstrations on their premises. These activities, and more, lead to organizational success.

Example of an Organization

The following are descriptions of two scenarios and how they achieved success. The pre- and post-state of each case is then explained.

Scenario 1 pre-exercise stage: An employee performance and rewards system was in place but was not in a standardized format.

Scenario 1 post-consultancy stage: A performance and reward system was standardized within the division; employee-engagements activities were implemented, such as a quality fair, a newsletter, and the use of tools such as kaizen and *Six Thinking Hats*; training development plans and a calendar were set up; induction programs were streamlined; feedback and assessment setups were gained from 3600 leaders; key result areas (KRAs) and key performance indicators (KPIs) were set up for the HR department; competency frameworks were put in place; and career progress plans were laid out. The impact included employee benefits, personal development, employee commitments and satisfaction, the institution of the HR department's basic operational requirements, and the implementation of leaders' individual development plans.

Scenario 2 pre-exercise stage: Strategic positioning (via the BSC) was ineffective or was communicated using KPIs (just a template).

Scenario 2 post-consultancy stage: The BSC was developed by considering the internal and external elements of the exercise—for example, by using various analyses such as Porter, PESTEL (political, economic, social, technological, legal, and environmental), SWOT (strengths, weaknesses, opportunities, and threats), and PRIMO-F (people, resources, information/ideas, marketing, operations, and finances)—process drafting was done, a process manual was developed, process improvement exercises were deployed, a risk management matrix was set up, and a sustainability policy was designed. The impact was that the performance improvement sustained outstanding results.

Some of the important lessons learned from these scenarios include the three Ds: discipline, diligence, and discernment. These factors make up the main fibers of the fabric of success. I have seen several organizations conceiving fantastic initiatives in order to attain their objectives. Yet, quite often these end up leaving the drawing board only to end up in the trash. To deploy the initiative to its successful completion calls for strong *discipline*—in keeping in mind the bigger picture at all times, in adhering to processes and frameworks established to propel actions in the right direction, and in the governance of each process.

Diligence will result in a doggedness that will propel all efforts toward the goalposts. Diligence implies a synergy of all initiatives that may be interlinked to achieve a common purpose. Gone are the times when it was all right to work in silos. Teamwork is now the name of the game. Thus, process linkages need to be understood, using a proactive approach, to make interdependent teams work together in synergy.

Discernment between short-term gains and long-term goals, between quality and cost, and between investment and divestment decisions—these and more are key to the successful attainment of objectives at the macro level. My advice here is to have the necessary internal discipline that will lead to the diligent dispersal of responsibilities. Take ownership, and do not hesitate to experiment. Follow your gut. Do the unconventional. Have the courage to innovate yourself in every new project you handle. Discern small gains that compromise long-term larger gains; keep the macro picture in your mind at all times, and do not allow yourself to be swerved from the path. Always stay focused on the bigger picture, and do not get lost in the myriad of operational chores. My advice for senior roles in the organization is to empower the team at all times so as to be able to chase the larger goals while entrusting the fragments to the team. Always be aware that some losses may occur while chasing bigger gains. Instill unfailing confidence in the team to be able to "make it good." Focus on the happiness of the team, as this will lead to organizational success at all times.

Quality Methodology

The European Foundation for Quality Management (EFQM) model is a holistic tool that takes into account practically every aspect of the business initiatives necessary to attain organizational goals. The tool's fundamental concepts are well integrated into the nine criteria that lead to business excellence. The EFQM is a well-rounded model that incorporates internal and external leadership; strategy conceptualization and deployment; process frameworks; product and service portfolio management; corporate governance; the optimization of human capital; and the effective utilization of financial strength, infrastructure, technology, and organizational knowledge. It triggers the need to develop a business model canvas that will put the entire organizational framework together on a single page.

The EFQM model is a results-driven framework that compels businesses to address the key success factors that will help to realize the vision of the organization. This focus on results leads to objectivity in the deployment of all initiatives across the length and breadth of the organization. The model brings out the interdependence between various functions and thus fosters internal collaboration.

Here is an example related to my company. EBM-BP was conceived due to the lack of benchmarking information in the region. There had been a total absence of any means of local comparisons in the UAE prior to the establishment of this program. We had no basis for relevant comparison in the UAE. Companies had to resort to expensive reports, several of which were rendered ineffective since the UAE has a special business environment, whether in terms of factors that affect business strategy, employee profiles, customer tendencies, or resource management.

The launch of EBM-BP has helped to not only provide businesses with relevant data for comparison but to also provide a valid rationale for realistic and structured target setting. This has created a new pathway to achieve growth, now with focus and purpose. The performance measures and indicators available through this program facilitate benchmarking and comparisons, both for target setting and for stimulating controlled business growth itself. The expanse of data covers everything: communication, employee engagement, teamwork, factual decision-making, process improvement, sound leadership, strategic intent, and more.

Perspective on Benchmarking

Benchmarking is not an end in itself. It is a means to the end—the end being continual improvement, ultimately driving toward business excellence. It is a method of making a structured comparison with other organizations with respect to their ideas, their processes, their best practices, and their data, with the sole purpose of understanding one's own strengths and areas for improvement, as well as finding appropriate changes that may be implemented in one's own organization in order to become more effective and efficient in driving results.

A focused leadership team empowered with the right human capital management initiatives is the key to the successful implementation of improvement initiatives in a business environment. Using a well-documented strategy that is driven using a BSC may prove to be an effective tool to drive this implementation. Using human capital to drive processes to the optimum will undoubtedly result in optimized customer experience. As noted earlier, however, clarity from the leadership team is what's really needed. Having that in place, steering the organization toward success should be easy using a set of systematic frameworks. Governance procedures may be implemented using the BSC while also addressing risk.

Now, to make a BSC work, one needs to set rational targets. These may be set using various inputs such as past performance, current macro-level organizational goals, available resources, market conditions, and, among other factors, benchmarking.

What do we mean by benchmarking? Benchmarking is a process that enables an organization to study industry data and to use that data as an internal gauge to measure itself against. The data should comprise the industry best, average, and worst performances. While this implies a study of numbers, benchmarking should not be restricted to numbers. It must also study the processes that lead to those numbers. Thus, holistic benchmarking entails the study of best practices, best-run processes, and the results of those practices and processes. The output of such a study will culminate in a plan to find ways to improve one's own organizational practices and processes, and ultimately raise the bar on the results as an outcome of such improvements. This exercise helps organizations to weed out the not-so-good practices, improve on what can be done better, and multiply their strengths by emulating the success stories of other organizations.

Typically, organizations will first conduct an internal exercise using existing popular tools such as SWOT and PRIMO-F in order to arrive at a list of problem areas. While SWOT will provide an overall perspective of the internal and external factors that affect the business, PRIMO-F will facilitate a detailed introspection into the internal business processes of an organization. Next, these problem areas may be prioritized using an *urgent–important matrix*, as shown in Table 9.1.

Table 9.1   Urgent–Important Matrix

		Urgency	
		High	*Low*
Importance	**High**	Highly urgent and highly important tasks	Highly important tasks with low urgency
	Low	Highly urgent tasks with low importance	Tasks that are neither urgent nor important

Once this clarity has been established, projects are defined and project teams are formed to address the problems. Each project team then studies the industry, with a view to comparing its own processes with those of the leading and successful businesses around them. Benchmarking one's own performance against that of another better performer is key to ongoing improvement. As noted earlier, benchmarking may be done within the region or within the industry. It may not always be done against the competition. Benchmarking needs to be understood for what it truly represents. While numbers contribute toward quantifiable comparisons, benchmarking should not be limited to numbers: the benchmarking of processes and initiatives is equally, if not more, important.

Benchmarking visits and sessions may be established to study the key success factors of competing businesses; internal changes may then be made to overcome any barriers to greater results. Thus, the process of benchmarking leads to greater organizational growth, without having to necessarily reinvent the wheel. Needless to say, industry-wide benchmarking is a great tool to bring about overall market improvement, thus uplifting the local economy itself.

Best Practices of Benchmarking in Organizations and Its Benefits

Organizations can use benchmarking for self-improvement and business excellence in many ways. Internal and external benchmarking are two methods; local and global benchmarking are two more. These may all be further categorized into industry-specific and non-industry-specific benchmarking. No matter which method one uses, one needs to be focused on the three Ds, as mentioned earlier: discipline, diligence, and discernment. These make up the main fibers of the fabric of success.

For any organization to deploy benchmarking, it is imperative that they use the three Ds as a basis for the project. It may not suffice to organize a benchmarking visit to an organization with the best practices. Strong discipline must be incorporated within the team to ensure that the existing processes are changed to bring about an improvement. Doing things in the same way as before cannot and will not bring about improvement, and the exercise of benchmarking would then be lost. As Einstein said, insanity is doing the same thing over and over again and expecting different results.

The EBM-BP program is a wonderful system that is locally available for organizations to share their data and processes in a transparent way. Since its inception in 2015, the program has facilitated the sharing of best practices in all areas of business excellence, including leadership, strategy, employees, partnerships, resource management, financial planning, sustainability, knowledge management, IT, process management, process improvement, product and service portfolio management, and customers, among others. During over 130 EBM Benchmarking Club sessions, the program has facilitated the sharing of best practices between over 400 corporate professionals. The EBM benchmarking visits have enabled nearly 100 corporate professionals to mingle freely with host organizations and to learn from their best practices.

Of course, the UAE has witnessed individual organizations making personal efforts to gather global benchmarks for industry-specific updates for those industries that do not offer enough local competition. In addition, local data for over sixty key performance measures (KPMs) has been facilitated by the EBM-BP program in a very short span of time.

Benchmarking has made a significant contribution toward helping organizations not only understand how they compare with the best in the region, but also to know the average performance of organizations in the region. The practice has helped companies to make proactive moves toward setting *stretch* targets and working toward attaining them. Over the years, organizations have been able to easily access the maximum, average, and minimum numbers for a wide range of customer, employee, process, IT, societal, financial, and other business-related KPMs for a very economical price and from the comfort of their own offices. The following hypothetical example (Table 9.2 and Figure 9.1) shows how data can be used to generate benchmarking information.

The process of active benchmarking through the EBM-BP program has had another significant positive outcome: that of unifying the calculation methodology for various KPMs. This unification has helped highlight the difference between the weighted average calculation method of perception measures

Table 9.2   Customer Perception Results: Satisfaction with Product/Service Quality

UAE Retailers	2011	2012	2013	2014	Average
Retailer 1	69.0	75.0	82.0	87.0	78.25
Retailer 2	87.0	86.0	88.0	90.0	87.75
Retailer 3	76.0	79.0	72.0	75.0	75.5
Retailer 4	95.0	93.0	96.0	98.0	95.5
My company	86.0	80.0	87.0	93.0	86.5
Retailer: highest	95.0	93.0	96.0	98.0	95.5
Retailer: average	82.6	82.6	85.0	88.6	84.7
Retailer: lowest	69.0	75.0	72.0	75.0	75.5

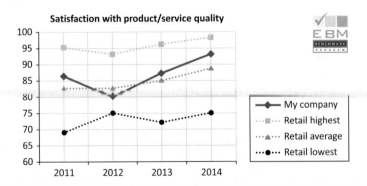

Figure 9.1   Satisfaction with product/service quality.

and the method of calculating using the number of positive responses received for perception surveys. Doing so has helped to make assessments more objective and accurate. Prior to this program, the two methods were not differentiated, and thus benchmarking was not comparable for the same KPMs.

The following example illustrates this situation very well. (The data and names are hypothetical.) We will study the difference between the overall customer satisfaction index (calculated using weighted averages) and the percentage of positive responses for customer satisfaction (calculated using the percentage of positive responses).

Scenario 1

We will show the results of scenario 1 using KRAs for customer perceptions, KPIs for overall customer satisfaction, and KPMs for the percentage of positive responses for customer satisfaction, as shown in Table 9.3.

Calculation Methodology

- Columns Q1 through Q5 represent the responses received on a five-point scale, where 5 is very satisfied, and 1 is very dissatisfied.
- Columns "Weighted Q1" through "Weighted Q5" represent the weighted scores from 5 to 1 for responses 5 to 1.
- The overall customer satisfaction index is calculated using the average score of all averages, across all questions (=4.38/5 in this example).
- The overall customer satisfaction index (percent) is a percentage of the overall customer satisfaction index (= [4.38/5]×100 in this example).

Scenario 2

Using the same data for scenario 2, we will again see the result using KRAs for customer perceptions, KPIs for overall

Table 9.3 Data Table for Scenario 1: Customer Satisfaction Factors (Q1–Q5)

#	Q1	Weighted Q1	Q2	Weighted Q2	Q3	Weighted Q3	Q4	Weighted Q4	Q5	Weighted Q5
1	5	5	5	5	5	5	5	5	4	4
2	5	5	3	3	5	5	4	4	5	5
3	5	5	5	5	3	3	5	5	4	4
4	5	5	4	4	5	5	5	5	3	3
5	5	5	3	3	4	4	2	2	5	5
6	5	5	5	5	5	5	5	5	5	5
7	5	5	5	5	1	1	3	3	5	5
8	5	5	4	4	5	5	5	5	3	3
9	5	5	5	5	5	5	5	5	5	5
10	5	5	4	4	4	4	2	2	4	4
Average score		5		4.3		4.2		4.1		4.3
Overall customer satisfaction index										4.38
Overall customer satisfaction index (%)										88%

customer satisfaction, and KPMs for the percentage of positive responses for customer satisfaction (Table 9.4).

Calculation Methodology

- Columns Q1 through Q5 represent the responses received on a five-point scale, where 5 is very satisfied, and 1 is very dissatisfied.
- +Resp is the number of positive responses received on a five-point scale, where 4 and 5 are positive and other values are not counted as positive.
- +Resp% is the percentage of positive responses received out of the total responses received (in this example, for Q3, eight out of ten responses are either 4 or 5).
- The percentage of positive responses for customer satisfaction is the average of +Resp%.

Table 9.4   Data Table for Scenario 2: Customer Satisfaction Factors (Q1–Q5)

#	Q1	Q2	Q3	Q4	Q5
1	5	5	5	5	4
2	5	3	5	4	5
3	5	5	3	5	4
4	5	4	5	5	3
5	5	3	4	2	5
6	5	5	5	5	5
7	5	5	1	3	5
8	5	4	5	5	3
9	5	5	5	5	5
10	5	4	4	2	4
+Resp.	10	8	8	7	8
+Resp.%	100%	80%	80%	70%	80%
% of positive responses for customer satisfaction					82%

As is evident, the EBM-BP program has helped to show the difference in the calculation methodology and to remove the differences in benchmarks for affected KPMs. Several member organizations of the EBM-BP program have successfully used this tool to streamline and align their data and to make accurate observations while planning their future actions for business improvement.

Taking Advantage of Benchmarking

Benchmarking is a tool that must be used with maturity. It is important for us not only to go about the process of benchmarking but also to know how to use the data to our advantage for continual improvement. I recommend you bear the following in mind while benchmarking:

- Understand your own data well, using the right method while number crunching; it is not as important to have great results as it is to have accurate results.
- Know your own process well prior to embarking on studying someone else's process.
- Always keep the context of your process in focus and remember your key objective at all times.
- Set realistic targets for improvement.
- Select your baseline data well in advance.
- Try to engage with as many process owners within your organization as possible, rather than engaging with only a select few. Often, the temptation is to cut costs and not include the larger team in the benchmarking exercise, but this may result in compromising on the benefits of an all-round study of the "best" process, by relevant process owners.
- Identify clearly *what* to benchmark and focus on using the information for setting rational targets for improvement.

- Actually, work toward making a positive change to your internal processes after having studied the benchmark process; without this important step, any benchmarking study is redundant.
- Rely on third-party benchmarking programs (e.g., the EBM-BP program) to ensure objective and reliable information sharing.
- Refrain from seeking to acquire commercially sensitive data from competitors and instead focus on business processes, HR practices, and the like.
- The benchmarking exercise may relate to technical, scientific, operational, or other initiatives that do not involve confidential price and related data, capacity or production data, cost data, profit margins, or sensitive marketing and sales information.
- Participation in the benchmarking exercise must be structured in such a way that information does not flow directly between participants but only through an independent third party.

I also recommend avoiding a few things while benchmarking:

- Don't benchmark for the sake of it.
- Don't lose sight of your goals; do not forget the bigger picture at any time.
- Get your senior management involved in the process of benchmarking so that you can get their total commitment toward putting improvement plans into action after the process.
- Benchmarking is a two-way exercise. Don't enter this neighborhood if you can't share your internal processes and data.
- Don't succumb to the lure of trying to prove that your processes are the best.
- Don't withhold your own information while benchmarking with others.

- Don't rest after benchmarking once. This is an ongoing process, and companies need to continuously update themselves to see continual improvement.
- Don't ignore the competition while benchmarking, under the assumption that you are better than them or that they won't be willing to share their information honestly with you.
- Don't compromise the data your benchmarking partner has shared in confidence.

Benchmarking enables organizations to handle the competition, opens up avenues of new ideas, and generally drives organizations toward continual business improvement. It is a structured exercise that results in the improved quality of products and services, reduced costs, and improved efficiency, among other benefits. Benchmarking brings about greater positive competitiveness in the business environment. Benchmarking also leads to data-based and fact-based discussions, rather than working on assumptions and gut feelings. It helps organizations to objectively analyze their internal performance, identify their own best practices, determine where their performance needs to be shaped up, and look for solutions to enhance their output. It triggers a continual improvement across all functions in the organization, and it often results in kaizen activities at all levels.

Performance benchmarking has several advantages. Performance may be of various types, spanning across numerous areas. Some of these are as follows:

- *Process performance*: This forces organizations to lose slack and to emerge from their comfort zones. Process improvement tools are put into action in order to improve turnaround times (TATs), make processes lean, and reduce the cost of doing things. Benchmarking their processes with the best in the region allows organizations to develop specific and measurable improvement plans based on the best practices of better-performing organizations, rather than being limited only to data of historical performance. Benchmarking removes the cobwebs from the internal system and makes way for new and innovative ideas for improvement.

■ *Product performance*: Benchmarking the product performance of competitors could lead to an overall product quality improvement. One common practice among manufacturers is to purchase competitors' products in order to study them and to try to understand how they outperform their own products. This leads to product design improvement. Overall, such actions benefit the entire industry at large, since they result in improved product quality for the consumer.

■ *Service performance*: Benchmarking the service performance of one's own organization against that of others helps to clearly identify improvement opportunities that can turn around customers and ultimately lead to greater market share. New service performance standards may be set, thus raising the bar of services rendered across all customer touch points, which in turn will ensure the utmost customer satisfaction. Since the change for improvement is triggered by an external organization, the change has a better chance of being accepted internally and thus has a greater chance of succeeding. This situation can also result in greater enthusiasm among staff members to work toward the successful implementation of new ideas, which will then foster greater teamwork.

Benchmarking may result in an increase in sales and overall productivity, and ultimately in an improved bottom line.

Chapter 10

Conclusion

Quality matters, even today! Quality professionals are challenged in several ways. Given that we now operate in a highly digitized world, it is imperative for us to think of new ways to think about quality. Quality plays a significant role in elevating an organization's performance, so quality experts have to find ways to continually evolve, to learn from good practices, and to build quality as a strategic differentiator for achieving superior performance.

By examining the experiences of several quality leaders, particularly from the UAE, we have extracted some of the ways to grow as leaders for quality, methodologies that are useful in certain settings, and the most exclusive lessons that our experts have learned on their quality journeys. From a leader's perspective, passion is key for quality. What is unique about quality leaders is their ability to envisage the gaps in the quality chain. As our key expert profiled in Chapter 9, Indu Singhal, puts it: "I see gaps in the system. Somehow, my eyes seem to be trained to pick them out. And my psyche does not permit me to ignore the gaps. Thus, I guess, it is my outlook that inspires me to be conscious of quality management, although I prefer to call it *business excellence*. This disposition helped me to conceptualize the local EBM-BP program, among other things." Truly, leaders need to have this kind of appetite for embracing quality.

Just as many leaders do, quality experts strongly believe in having a continuous focus on the customer. Given that we have created a strong foundation for a digitalized world, customer care has become even more crucial. Our expert Raju Ravi Prakash recalled that "the customer is the king. Repeat orders can only be received if the delivery of the product is to the customer's satisfaction by doing the job right the first time." If such continuity is to be maintained, quality professionals indeed face a huge challenge. Embracing this challenge is the future of quality.

Our quality experts have illustrated that it is hard to specify which methodology is best or what tools are key to achieving quality. This is because, while the basics remain the same, each of the methodologies or models are applied differently and will have different results and consequences in different contexts. Our quality experts believe that ISO standards are very efficient improvement tools, especially when coupled with the implementation of Lean programs. Some of the tools that quality experts use include (1) the quality management methodologies originated by and included in Six Sigma; (2) the quality assurance methodologies used in the automotive sector, such as QFD, FMEA, and AQAP; and (3) quality control statistical tools for product and process control, measurement, and the enhancement of process performance and capabilities, such as X-R charts, Cp, Cpk, and DOE.

Quality positions are key to achieving operational excellence, however, and our experts have a message for quality professionals. For example, Prakash asserts this key message: "I strongly believe that the word *fail* stands for 'first attempt in learning.'" It is obvious that quality professionals should thoroughly embrace failures and work on them. Another key message that has emerged from our quality experts is to embrace the fact that quality is everybody's business. It is extremely important to thoroughly understand the requirements of the customer and to deliver the product without compromising on quality. The maintenance of records with meaningful information is crucial, as the objective evidence helps to sort out many issues during the handling of a project.

Our expert Nancy Nouaimeh further observed that the quality profession is extremely valuable to any business and to its growth and sustainability, and our roles may evolve significantly in the future, as the current research shows. The need for a quality mind-set to focus efforts on a company's required improvements will likely grow even larger in the future. Quality tools and methodologies will be very useful in areas such as innovation and sustainability, where structured approaches and measurements are needed to demonstrate the effectiveness of new ideas and to determine their impacts both before and after implementation. Ultimately, dedication and commitment to quality are the key to success. One of the study participant said that "if you do it with passion, the quality will be there, as I believe that anything that has been done with passion and love will also generate quality."

Our experts advise the leaders of organizations to find ways to make quality a strategic priority. Hence, they assert that leaders have to understand that everyone is important in an organization. The involvement of people using an open-minded approach is a healthy sign for any company's success. The introduction of reward and recognition will bring fame and will motivate employees to do better. Companies must strongly discourage the blame culture from developing.

Quality professionals must embrace several important skills. Speaking of skills, Singhal says that there is no single skill that quality professionals must develop: "I swear by the three Ds. Having said that, one really needs to work toward having a cauldron of knowledge, passion, and relationship management. Integrity must be the backbone of every action to make it reach its logical conclusion. Speaking of today's business environment, I do not find it complex at all. Complexities are the drama of a certain mind-set. We have to unshackle our minds and open up to the sea of solutions for any given solution. Creativity and innovation are everybody's business; it is not limited to a select team in an organization. We have to trigger our inner cells to churn out new ways of doing things. Personally, I have a daily target in my mind to do at least one thing in a different way, no matter how small and seemingly insignificant. It keeps my fire burning."

Needless to say, quality professionals must have a clear appetite for improvement and learning. Given the depth of the challenges quality professionals face, they have to be able to meet these requirements and to be successful in the quality vision of their organizations. Specifically, new professionals should work in cross-functional departments and projects and should work toward understanding the overall processes of any organization they serve. One of our experts has also said, taking this kind of initiative will help new employees to understand quality from different perspectives in order to design meaningful solutions to the industry or organization in today's complex environment.

With exceptional curiosity, dedication, and passion for quality, one can emerge as a leader for quality. In doing so, young experts can ponder the following questions:

1. What does *leadership/strategy for quality* mean to us?
2. How can we describe the best practices of our organization by showcasing the leadership and strategy in the organization?
3. How do we think the leadership and strategy have helped the organization to achieve a deep-rooted quality culture in the organization?
4. What are examples of results or organizational performance that resulted from good leadership and strategy implementation?
5. What things would have gone wrong if the leadership or strategy had not functioned well in the organization?
6. What does the *involvement of people* mean to us?

7. Can you describe the best practices and approaches of your organization, showcasing the organization's *involvement of people* principle?
8. How can you describe some of the results you have obtained for the *people enabler* in your organization or in any organization that is known to you?
9. What are the unique ways that your organization leverages the people enabler?
10. How are we leveraging our process to gain maximum benefit?

Finally, good practices are just base points to begin the journey, but to mature in excellence, organizations have to keep their quality efforts highly relevant, current, and, most importantly, modern to cope with the ever-changing business environment. A whole approach to quality in the twenty-first century will have to find new ways of engaging customers and people and leveraging all other stakeholders by considering the digitized world we live in. We have to take full advantage of this mega-trend of digitization!

Index

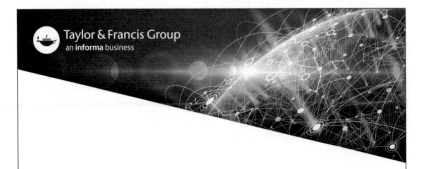

Taylor & Francis eBooks

www.taylorfrancis.com

A single destination for eBooks from Taylor & Francis
with increased functionality and an improved user
experience to meet the needs of our customers.

90,000+ eBooks of award-winning academic content in
Humanities, Social Science, Science, Technology, Engineering,
and Medical written by a global network of editors and authors.

TAYLOR & FRANCIS EBOOKS OFFERS:

A streamlined
experience for
our library
customers

A single point
of discovery
for all of our
eBook content

Improved
search and
discovery of
content at both
book and
chapter level

REQUEST A FREE TRIAL
support@taylorfrancis.com

Routledge
Taylor & Francis Group

CRC Press
Taylor & Francis Group